LAN
ZAR
OTE

**Travel with Marco Polo
Insider Tips**

INSIDER TIP
**Your shortcut
to a great
experience**

MARCO POLO
TOP HIGHLIGHTS

JAMEOS DEL AGUA ⭐
Semi-open caves transform into a spectacular landscape artwork. The rare white crab is at home in the underground lake.
📷 *Tip: It's at its best when the bright entrance is reflected in the water of the lake.*

➤ p. 56, Costa Teguise & the North

CUEVA DE LOS VERDES ⭐
Enjoy a mysterious journey to the underworld: an empty lava tube leads deep into the heart of the volcano.
📷 *Tip: The best sights will be brought to your attention – but the best is saved till last!*

➤ p. 57, Costa Teguise & the North

FUNDACIÓN CÉSAR MANRIQUE ⭐
The good life in lava bubbles – bright, cheerful and hip! The polymath's former house is now also a gallery.

➤ p. 54, Costa Teguise & the North

JARDÍN DE CACTUS ⭐
Prickly! 1,500 cacti growing in a former quarry.
📷 *Tip: The windmill at the garden's edge is best photographed in the late afternoon!*

➤ p. 55, Costa Teguise & the North

TEGUISE ⭐
White walls and wide squares meet churches and monasteries. Take a stroll through Lanzarote's former capital and be transported back in time.

➤ p. 60, Costa Teguise & the North

LA GERIA

Thousands of grass-green vines in troughs of black ash. The contrasts are astounding in the world's strangest wine landscape.

📷 *Tip: Focus on a few of the hollows for an abstract shot.*

➤ p. 79, Puerto del Carmen & the Centre

RUTA DE LOS VOLCANES ⭐

The bus tour through the strange landscape of the national park is as otherworldly as a trip to the moon.

➤ p. 100, Timanfaya National Park & the South

CHARCO DE LOS CLICOS ⭐

Find yourself in a sci-fi film location – the poison-green sea-water lagoon of a volcanic crater.

📷 *Tip: Take a photo from El Golfo where you can capture the lake, sea and volcano from up high.*

➤ p. 95, Timanfaya National Park & the South

PLAYAS DE PAPAGAYO ⭐

The golden-yellow "parrot beaches" are the island's most beautiful (photo).

➤ p. 93, Timanfaya National Park & the South

SALINAS DE JANUBIO ⭐

The salt pans resemble a giant chessboard. Try their crowning glory, the *flor de sal*.

📷 *Tip: At sunset, the salt flats transform into gigantic, shimmering discs.*

➤ p. 95, Timanfaya National Park & the South

CONTENTS

COSTA TEGUISE
& THE NORTH

PUERTO DEL CARMEN
& THE CENTRE

ARRECIFE

TIMANFAYA NATIONAL PARK
& THE SOUTH

36   REGIONAL OVERVIEW

38   ARRECIFE

**48   COSTA TEGUISE
& THE NORTH**

Costa Teguise & around   52
La Graciosa   58
Teguise & around   60

**70   PUERTO DEL CARMEN
& THE CENTRE**

Puerto del Carmen & around   74

**84   TIMANFAYA
NATIONAL PARK
& THE SOUTH**

Playa Blanca & around   88
Parque Nacional de Timanfaya   98

CONTENTS

MARCO POLO TOP HIGHLIGHTS
2 Top 10 highlights

BEST OF LANZAROTE
8 ... when it rains
9 ... on a budget
10 ... with children
11 ... classic experiences

GET TO KNOW LANZAROTE
14 Discover Lanzarote
17 At a glance
18 Understanding Lanzarote
21 True or false?

EATING, SHOPPING, SPORT
26 Eating & drinking
30 Shopping
32 Sport & activities

MARCO POLO REGIONS
36 Regional overview

DISCOVERY TOURS
102 Lanzarote at a glance
108 Desert landscapes &
monasteries: cycling around
El Jable

110 A hike through seas of lava
112 Meet the neighbours: head to
Fuerteventura!

GOOD TO KNOW

116 **HOLIDAY BASICS**
*Arrival, Getting around,
Emergencies, Essentials,
Festivals & events, Weather*

124 **USEFUL WORDS & PHRASES**
*There's no need to be lost for
words*

126 **HOLIDAY VIBES**
Books, films, music & blogs

128 **TRAVEL PURSUIT**
The Marco Polo holiday quiz

130 **INDEX & CREDITS**

132 **DOS & DON'TS**
*How to avoid slip-ups &
blunders*

☉	Plan your visit	🍴	Eating/drinking	🌂	Rainy day activities
€–€€€	Price categories	🛍	Shopping	🦬	Budget activities
(*)	Premium-rate phone number	❖	Going out	🐒	Family activities
		⛱	Top beaches	⚑	Classic experiences

(𝄃𝄃 A2) Refers to the removable pull-out map
(0) Located off the map

BEST OF
LANZAROTE

Fine sand, gentle waves: Playa Papagayo is one of the island's top beaches

BEST

WHEN IT RAINS

ACTIVITIES TO BRIGHTEN YOUR DAY

STARK CONTRASTS

Explore art under barrel vaults in the dark corridors of the *Castillo de San José*, where the brightly coloured, classical modernist paintings really come into their own. Afterwards, you can enjoy a bite to eat in the panorama restaurant high above the harbour.

➤ p. 44, Arrecife

EYE TO EYE WITH A SHARK

The 2-m-long nurse shark Conan and a 1.5-m stingray patrol the large overhead tank at *Lanzarote Aquarium* in Costa Teguise. There are also totally harmless sea cucumbers, clownfish and spider crabs.

➤ p. 52, Costa Teguise & the North

CAVE LABYRINTH

Let your imagination run wild and step back in time to when people sheltered from pirates in the caverns of *Cueva de los Verdes*. To top off the experience, you'll also get an idea of the immense power unleashed by flowing lava.

➤ p. 57, Costa Teguise & the North

DIVE DEEP

If the sun's not shining, you may as well get totally soaked. Try a *submarine* diving tour for fascinating glimpses of marine life at a depth of 30m. Excursions start from Puerto Calero, among other places.

➤ p. 78, Puerto del Carmen & the Centre

AN EMOTIONAL ROLLER-COASTER

You will need several hours to sample the many stations in the Roman-inspired *bathing complex* at the hotel *Costa Calero* in Puerto Calero: from a music pool to various saunas and the warm thalasso spa bath with massage.

➤ p. 78, Puerto del Carmen & the Centre

BEST 🐷
ON A BUDGET

FOR SMALLER WALLETS

APPRECIATE THE ART
The *Casa de Cultura Agustín de la Hoz* in Arrecife not only exhibits art but is itself well worth a visit, featuring a delightful patio with a rather whimsically carved flight of steps and an early mural by César Manrique celebrating rural life – plus, admission is free!
➤ p. 42, Arrecife

GIVE ALOE VERA A TRY
You can taste *free samples of aloe cake and liqueur* at the *Lanzaloe* plantation without having to make a purchase (photo).
➤ p. 58, Costa Teguise & the North

FOR THE SURE-FOOTED
There is normally an admission charge to see César Manrique's landscape artworks, such as the *Mirador del Río*, the viewing platform over the straits between Lanzarote and the neighbouring island of La Graciosa. Just as spectacular, but free, is the view from the *Mirador de Guinate* and, what's more, it's quite likely that you will have the place to yourself.
➤ p. 68, Costa Teguise & the North

A LESSON IN VULCANOLOGY
The *visitor centre* at Timanfaya National Park impresses with a fascinating multimedia introduction to the geology of volcanoes.
➤ p. 100, Timanfaya National Park & the South

HIKES WITH A VIEW & LOCAL FACTS
National park rangers offer free walking tours from the *Centro de Visitantes Mancha Blanca* into the Fire Mountains and past craters, lava tubes and a solidified lava lake, and will reveal (in English) how they were formed.
➤ p. 101, Timanfaya National Park & the South

FEED THE ANIMALS

Granja las Pardelas, near Órzola, is a small petting zoo with goats, rabbits, donkeys and a horse. Donkey rides are offered and kids can create their own piece of pottery to remember the day.

➤ p. 58, Costa Teguise & the North

PIRATE FOR THE DAY

You'll think of knights and brigands as soon as you see Teguise's fortress and, once inside, the *Museo de la Piratería* will bring to life the times when pirates raided the island.

➤ p. 62, Costa Teguise & the North

WILDLIFE & MORE

Parrots, raptors and sea lions perform tricks at *Rancho Texas Lanzarote Park* in Puerto del Carmen. You can also find yourself at the heart of a Western with a hunt for gold and a cowboy night.

➤ p. 77, Puerto del Carmen & the Centre

SPLASH & SLIDE

Water slides, wet castles, a lazy river and artificial waves: Playa Blanca's *Aqualava Waterpark* is a paradise for water lovers.

➤ p. 91, Timanfaya National Park & the South

BOAT TOURS

Children love a trip out to sea – as long as it's not too long! The harbour of Playa Blanca is the starting point for a number of *boat trips*. The best is the glass-bottom boat which offers a glimpse into the underwater world. Ahoy there!

➤ p. 91, Timanfaya National Park & the South

DESERT RIDES

Hitch a ride through the Fire Mountains on one of the camels from the *dromedary station (Echadero de los Camellos)*.

➤ p. 99, Timanfaya National Park & the South

BEST

CLASSIC EXPERIENCES

BEASTLY RED

That crimson colour in lipstick or the red Campari in your glass: it all comes from the blood of the cochineal beetle, a bug that has made itself at home on Lanzarote's prickly pears.

➤ p. 20, Understand Lanzarote

BEAUTY FROM THE BOWELS OF THE EARTH

If you are taking a stroll on one of Lanzarote's lava-strewn beaches, lookout for pieces of *olivine*: a semi-precious, olive-green gemstone with a mysterious glow (photo).

➤ p. 31, Shopping

OLD SOUNDS, NEW TIMPLES

The *timple* arrived on the island with the African slaves, its bright sound an essential part of the Lanzarotean folk song. The stringed instrument is crafted by hand in small workshops, such as the one run by *Antonio Lemes Hernández*. In the *Casa-Museo del Timple* next door, you can hear it being played.

➤ p. 64 and p. 65, Costa Teguise & the North

SALT FROM SUN & SEA

Sea salt is harvested in the *Salinas de Janubio*, where you can buy it cheaply at the *Bodega de Janubio*. Traditional dishes, seasoned with *flor de sal*, the delicately flavoured "flower of salt", can be enjoyed nearby at *Mirador Las Salinas Casa Domingo* – an amazing place to watch the sun set over the shimmering pools of salt!

➤ p. 95, Timanfaya National Park & the South

LAVA BBQ, ANYONE?

The upward heat from the earth will barbecue crispy and tender meat all by itself! Try it yourself at *El Diablo* in the national park.

➤ p. 101, Timanfaya National Park & the South

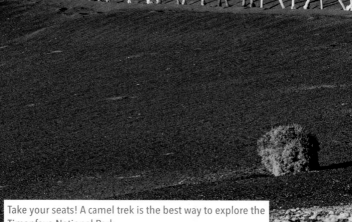

GET TO
KNOW
LANZAROTE

Take your seats! A camel trek is the best way to explore the Timanfaya National Park

DISCOVER LANZAROTE

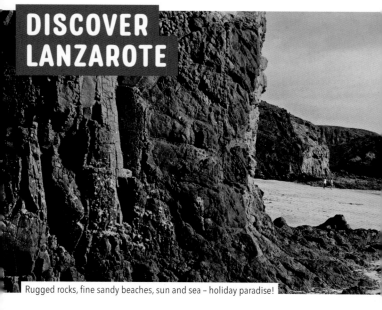

Rugged rocks, fine sandy beaches, sun and sea – holiday paradise!

Look out the window as your plane descends; it's as if you are arriving on the set for a science-fiction film. Suddenly, emerging from a steel-blue sea, is this picture of bare, beige-grey hills, black fields of lava and craters, a lunar landscape onto which scudding clouds cast their shadows, while the surging spray of the ocean showers over its shores.

A GLIMPSE INSIDE THE EARTH

At first sight an inhospitable wasteland, Lanzarote is quite different to the rest of the Canary Islands. A good 20 million years ago, huge volumes of basalt magma broke through the fault lines in the Earth's crust to form the two oldest islands in the archipelago, Fuerteventura and Lanzarote. Since then, the Canaries have

From 500 BCE – Berbers settle Lanzarote

1312 – A Genoese navigator, Lancelotto Malocello, lands on the island. Lanzarote later takes its name from him

1402 – The Norman Jean de Béthencourt conquers Lanzarote for the Castilian crown, and subjugates the aboriginal population

1730–36 and 1824 – Volcanic eruptions devastate the south of Lanzarote. Many emigrate to Latin America

1852 – Arrecife becomes the island's capital

1936 – A coup led by General Franco, the military commander of the Canary

never been totally free of seismic activity, and none of the other islands has seen so much volcanic turbulence as Lanzarote. Over 20 per cent of the island's surface (795km²), buried until 1736, was reshaped by lava and ash.

BLACK, WHITE & GREEN

It is this seemingly barren wasteland that makes Lanzarote unique. The volcanic heart of the island is an unparalleled spectacle of the natural world and a distinctive island feature – just like the pretty villages with white façades and green windows and doors. The fact that so many settlements radiate in these striking classic colours is due to the work of Lanzarote's most famous son, César Manrique. No other island in the archipelago can boast as many pieces of (landscape) art by the great painter, sculptor and architect as this land of volcanic fire.

BEACHES GALORE

Of course you don't have to spend your holiday immersed in culture, even though it is spectacular on Lanzarote. The alternative is called *Vamos a la Playa!* Swimming, snorkelling, relaxing under palm trees – all year round! All three major holiday resorts – Costa Teguise, Puerto del Carmen and Playa Blanca – have good beaches with soft white sand, in part protected by wave breakers. If you prefer something more active, you can dive, surf or fly across the water on a jet ski. The island's well-developed water-sports infrastructure provides equipment and instruction. Less athletic tourists can watch Lanzarote's coastline

Islands, triggers the three-year Spanish Civil War

1960 onwards – Tourism replaces agriculture as the island's main business

1975 – Following Franco's death, democratic government is restored to Spain; tourism takes off

1986 – Spain becomes a member of the European Community

1993 – UNESCO awards Biosphere Reserve status to Lanzarote

2010-17 – The global financial and economic crisis hits Spain hard. Tourism helps the Canary Islands to stage a recovery

glide by from a boat. The year-round mild temperatures encourage tourists to enjoy outdoor activities off the water as well. Road bikers love Lanzarote because

INSIDER TIP
Moon walk

it is relatively flat but diverse. And the volcanic mountains draw a surprising number of hikers – the lack of vegetation does not seem to bother them.

The mild climate is attributable to the northeast trade winds, which deliver rain to the other islands in the archipelago. Lanzarote's bad luck is that the highest peak, Peñas del Chache in the northern Risco de Famara range, is only 671m high, too low to trigger proper rainfall from the clouds. But the clouds, which can form dense clusters on the mountains, do help to moderate the heat, as does the Canary Current, a coolish reverse flow in the Gulf Stream system.

AFRICAN ROOTS

Little is known about the island's original inhabitants, the Majos. They probably came to Lanzarote from North Africa in the fifth century BCE or later and are genetically related to the light-skinned Berber peoples who still live there. The Majos lived from fishing and growing cereals, which were ground in primitive mills into *gofio* (see p. 26). They also bred sheep and goats. Nowadays, however, it would be impossible for the *Lanzaroteños* to live off farming and fishing alone.

TOURISM PAYS THE BILLS

Most of the 142,000 inhabitants earn their living from the two million holiday-makers who come to the island every year. Many local people work as receptionists, cooks, porters, cleaners, gardeners or travel guides – often as seasonal workers under precarious conditions. The island itself has had to come to grips with the increasing numbers of tourists. The wells ran dry a long time ago, so desalination plants now supply the island's drinking water. However, this has to be extracted and transported, which doesn't come cheap in terms of energy use. Wind farms reach up to the sky, strips of asphalt snake through the fields of lava. Over the course of just a few years, the small fishing village of Playa Blanca has been transformed into a mega-holiday resort, while holiday settlements for wealthy central Europeans have mushroomed.

Only in hidden corners, in villages well away from the main holiday centres, does one get the sense that Lanzarote, more so than all the other Canary Islands, is still a place of privation, repose and tranquillity. This can often be seen in the faces of the older rural population: farmers with a mule-drawn plough stoically turning over the dusty soil; farmers' wives harvesting fruit from endless rows of prickly pears; old men gathered in the village square idly passing the time of day. The Lanzarote of yesteryear lives on only here, and only those who go in search of it with open eyes and receptive ears, pausing as they look and listen, will discover the island's true magic.

AT A GLANCE

141,000 islanders
Isle of Wight: 141,600

NARROWEST POINT
20km

326km coastline
Mainland UK coastline: 17,819km

846km^2 area
Orkney Islands: 990km^2

TALLEST MOUNTAIN: PEÑAS DEL CHACHE
671m
summit not accessible – restricted military zone

YOUNG VOLCANOES COVER
172 KM^2
OF THE ISLAND

MOST POPULAR MONTH TO TRAVEL
DECEMBER

APPROX. **20** PLANTS ARE ENDEMIC TO THE ISLAND

This is the only place they exist in the world

ARRECIFE
is the capital with a population of 56,000

A Lanzarote camel or, more precisely, dromedary costs over 3,000 euro

HIGHEST BUILDING
The 17-storey Gran Hotel Arrecife

UNDERSTAND LANZAROTE

TOURIST VEHICLES

It is a truly amazing sight: long caravans picking their way slowly across the ash mountains in the Timanfaya National Park. Lanzarote's dromedaries are among the island's main tourist attractions. These single-humped beasts of burden almost certainly arrived on the island with the first Europeans. They make perfect working animals, as they can, if necessary, go for weeks without water and will carry heavy loads over long distances without complaint. They were used in the fields, to carry goods and to operate *gofio* mills, and can also be ridden like a horse.

It was thought that the introduction of the combustion engine on the island would end the careers of these frugal four-legged helpers. But tourism has given the dromedaries a new lease of life. Now, every day, hundreds of holidaymakers climb into the saddle on the side of the hump and take a rocking ride through the Fire Mountains in Timanfaya. Dromedaries are bred near the village of Uga. Every afternoon between 3pm and 4pm the weary caravan heads home from the national park – photo essential!

RABBIT ISLAND

The islanders categorically refuse to be lumped together with their brothers and sisters from the Spanish mainland. "We are Canarians," they will tell anyone who is willing to listen. "We speak, feel and act differently to them!" The feeling is definitely mutual. Many on the Spanish mainland not only agree with this, they also ascribe a multitude of unflattering attributes to the inhabitants of the far-away Canary Islands. Canarians are truly a breed of their own: a blend of nationalities that has developed over many hundreds of years and includes indigenous Berber people and Spanish conquistadors, Portuguese settlers and African slaves. Just as the archipelago sets great store by its distinctiveness, so the inhabitants of each of the islands celebrate that which makes them special.

And this certainly also includes nicknames: the Lanzaroteños, for example, call themselves *Conejeros*, which can be roughly translated as "those of the rabbit island". The name goes back to a period when the new Spanish owners of the island released rabbits on the desert island for hunting. Wild rabbits may be just a distant memory now, but the nickname has stuck. And it is used with pride: no matter whether it is a bodega, restaurant or car rental company, *"Los Conejeros"* (pronounced: "kone-heros") is a popular addition to any company name.

ONE HUNDRED PER CENT CLEAN

Better late than never: nature conservation is very much alive on the Canary Islands. The small island of La Graciosa off the northern coast of Lanzarote has sun, wind and (sea)

Two-wheeled transport on La Graciosa

water in abundance, which makes it the perfect place to implement a project to meet all power and water needs with renewable sources. Co-funded by the EU, the *Microred La Graciosa* project is working to take the 500 islanders off the grid *(www. lagraciosadigitalocho.blogspot.com)*.

PERFECTLY ADAPTED

At first sight Lanzarote might seem totally lifeless. But, if you look closely enough, thousands of wild plants, many of which only occur on the Canary Islands, can be found growing on the island. These include the spring-flowering, white *tajinaste* (bugloss), the scented, lavender-like *retama* and the sweet and bitter *tabaibas*, squat bushes that defy the blistering sun and strong winds with their fleshy, water-storing branches. Hundreds of types of lichen have invaded the lava, breaking down the once-molten rock in a process that takes millennia. The *cardón* is the best-known of the many varieties of euphorbia. Its long, spiny columns tower skyward like candelabra. Canarian date palms, whose over-hanging foliage and orange-coloured fruit give the valley around Haría a distinctive African feel, are plants that only thrive on the Canary Islands.

But the weirdest of them is all is the *drago*, the dragon tree, that on Lanzarote only grows in gardens. For the early Canarians the dragon tree, with its scaly bark, thick, bizarrely shaped branches with clusters of sabre-like leaves and a tail of cherry-sized fruit, was regarded as sacred because

This wool gets its bright red colour from the cochineal beetle

of its precious resin. Known as dragon's blood, this fluid turns dark red when exposed to the air. It was used from early times in the preparation of medicinal potions and ointments.

BEETLY COLOUR

Many people think it's some sort of bad joke, but it's true: the striking red colouring of Campari comes from beetle blood. If you are not convinced, you can check it out for yourself on Lanzarote. Growing on the many acres of land between Guatiza and Mala is an abundance of prickly (or cactus) pears. The plant's Latin name is *Opuntia* and it is native to Mexico, but it is also the favourite food of the cochineal beetle. And this scale insect, just a few millimetres long and barely larger than a match head, produces a deep crimson colour.

The bugs, released on the cactus leaves, feed on the plant's sap and multiply rapidly. They excrete a soft, white, powdery substance that is plain to see on the cactus leaves. Every two to three months, the bugs are removed manually from the prickly *Opuntia* plants using a scraper. When they have been cleaned, they are killed by immersion in hot water, dried and ground. Millions of the insects die to make a kilo of cochineal dye.

After the invention of cheap, synthetic aniline dyes, prospects for the once lucrative cochineal business started to fade. Natural cochineal red is still used in some foods (sweets, liqueurs), cosmetics and medicines. Products made using cochineal, e.g. soaps, bath essences and peeling masks, may be purchased in Punta

Mujeres at *Aloe Vera House (Mon–Sat 10am–6pm, Sun 10am–5pm | C/ Jameos del Agua 2 | www.aloeplus lanzarote.com).*

Since 2016, *"Cochinilla de Canarias"* is allowed to bear the EU label "protected designation of origin" (PDO). This confirms its originality: the beetle species, its cactus host plant and the natural production process are unique in Europe.

DO NO HARM!

Lucha canaria or *Canarian wrestling* has been a popular pursuit on the island since the days of the early Canarians. The sport is only practised on the islands of the Canarian archipelago, and thrilling contests are still popular today. A team consists of twelve wrestlers, but they only fight in pairs within a ring 12m in diameter and covered with sawdust or sand.

Battle commences from a starting position, i.e. leaning forward facing the opponent with their trouser leg in the left hand. Each contest lasts a maximum of three minutes. The *luchadores*, as the wrestlers are known, grasp their opponent using a variety of holds, the object being to floor him/her. But what is required is not just strength. Technique and speed are also decisive. There are no weight categories. Thus, it is possible for a 55kg lightweight to be facing a colossus weighing twice as much. Women are also involved in the sport. If an opponent is floored twice in a maximum of three fights, then the victor wins a point and the defeated wrestler has to drop out. The team that still has

TRUE OR FALSE?

THE SAND IS BLACK

Everything is volcanic, so the lava beaches must be dark too, right? Think again! The sea plays a part too, creating stunning sandy white beaches from the skeletons of sea animals which the surf has ground into the finest sand. Hence the sand at the Playas de Papagayo and Puerto del Carmen and Órzola. So not all the sand is dark…

WATCH OUT FOR THE VOLCANOES

The last time there was an eruption on Lanzarote was in 1824 and further west on El Hierro in 2011. Luckily, there was plenty of warning prior to the eruptions. Geologists say future volcanic activity is possible, but they don't know when. It could be 1,000, 100 or just two years away. For this reason, even the smallest of tremors is recorded so that, in the case of an eruption, everyone is evacuated in time.

THE SPANISH EAT SO LATE!

At the time we sit down to eat in the UK, the Lanzarote locals are just having a *merienda* – a snack – at the most. Dinner is usually served around 10pm, followed by a quick walk to aid digestion before bed. Unless it's the weekend … when night carries on until day!

wrestlers on the bench at the end wins the competition.

Should you wish to be a spectator at a Canarian wrestling match and experience the atmosphere in the audience, there are arenas *(terrero de lucha)* in Tinajo, Uga, Yaiza, Playa Blanca and Tahiche. The competitions are usually held at the weekend, but an up-to-date listing of events is available from the tourist information office or you can visit *www.federacion deluchacanariadelanzarote.com*.

JACK OF ALL TRADES

Was there anything this Arrecife-born polymath couldn't do? Painter, sculptor, architect, designer, writer and green activist, César Manrique, born in 1919, was successful in many fields and is, by a long way, Lanzarote's most famous son.

After his first exhibitions of representational pictures, in 1945 he moved to Madrid, where he discovered abstract art and quickly made a name for himself. In 1965 he left for the USA where he stayed for three years. But when the tourists started arriving on Lanzarote in 1968, he returned, so that he could be in a position to contribute artistically when the modern world reached his homeland. Fascinated by the island's nature, he strove to shine light on its beauty with as little intervention as possible. These days, he would be dubbed a minimalist, but one for whom anything angular or cold was alien. Instead, he embraced organic forms and "warm" natural materials such as volcanic stone and wood,

transforming tunnels of lava and caves into breathtakingly beautiful dreamscapes, and building monuments and wind chimes. But the artist was also a fighter who campaigned vigorously against a replication of the concrete monstrosities that had sprung up on the other Canary Islands. What he fought really hard for was the preservation of the island's landscape by promoting its traditional architecture. Against all odds, he persuaded the authorities to impose strict conditions; he designed low-rise holiday villages himself and oversaw the conversion of hotels.

Manrique died in a car accident on 25 September 1992 near his home at Tahiche. But the foundation which bears his name, the *Fundación César Manrique (www.fcmanrique. org)*, ensures that his "critical voice" continues to be heard. The exhibitions and workshops staged there address a wide range of topics, from art and architecture to globalisation, immigration, environmental protection and nature conservation. The foundation has set up museums in Manrique's former residences in Tahiche and Haría, which are worth visiting just to appreciate the architecture. His house in Tahiche (see p. 54), which is built within volcanic bubbles, is particularly interesting.

THIRST QUENCHER

Volcanoes, ash and sand plains are everywhere, while rain and ground water are scarce. So who quenches the thirst of the hotel gardens, golf courses and vineyards of the 140,000 inhabitants and over two million visitors? Water is the scarcest and most precious commodity on Lanzarote. In the past, the islanders took their drinking water from wells, fed from the Famara mountains along a system of long tunnels *(galerías)* to the settlements where it was needed, or else they collected rainwater in cisterns. The largest of these underground reservoirs, the *gran mareta*, was in Teguise. Everything changed in the early 1960s, a time when dromedaries were still pulling the ploughs on Lanzarote's fields and farmers were bringing in small harvests. One day, Manuel Díaz Rijo, manager of the Bodega Mozaga, had a bold idea. As part of his work as a marine engineer, he had been developing a system to remove salt from seawater so that ships' crews would no longer be dependent upon fresh water. Now he asked himself: wasn't the island itself pretty much a ship lying at anchor in the Atlantic? And so he designed the first seawater desalination plant for Lanzarote – it was inaugurated in 1965. From that day on, periods of drought ceased to be life-threatening.

Today's seawater desalination plants use osmosis, a method by which salt is removed from the ocean by means of a purely mechanical process that conserves resources. Moreover, wastewater treatment plants have been built to recycle used water and all large hotels are required to have their own seawater desalination plants.

Hidden behind this decorative wall in Tahíce is César Manrique's house

EATING SHOPPING SPORT

You'll find colourful curios at Lanzarote's markets

EATING & DRINKING

It is often said that Canarian food lacks sophistication. But the islanders have honed their inventive skills over the years, in order to conjure up a delicious meal using very little – and it's precisely this that has shaped the islanders' cuisine. The Lanzaroteans have had to overcome many hardships in their long history. No one could deny that. And, in spite of the dry soil and scorching sun, they have always managed to put food on the table. The fact is Canarian cuisine grew out of poverty.

LONG-TIME ALL-ROUNDER

Lanzarote's indigenous inhabitants survived mainly on *gofio*, a flour produced from roasted grains of barley or maize. First the grains were crushed and later ground into flour in windmills. The beige or light-brown powder had a long shelf-life, was versatile, rich in protein and filling. The Majos always kept a sack of *gofio* in the kitchen and with it they created a wide range of dishes: it was baked into bread, stirred into soup and drinks, added to fish, meat or potatoes or mixed with honey and almonds as a dessert. Daily life without *gofio* was unimaginable. It is still produced and served up at the table, but nowadays the powder is made from wheat or maize.

SOUPS & STEWS

Soups and stews have retained their status as everyday fare. A *potaje*, that famous vegetable soup into which the cook stirred anything that grew, is still to be found on the menu in every restaurant that serves home cooking. *Puchero* and *rancho canario* are heartier stews that contain chicken, beef or pork. Not to be forgotten is the *ropa vieja*, literally *old clothes*. The name quaintly, but clearly, refers to the

Fried calamari (left); *bienmesabe* (right)

origins of this country delicacy, i.e. the week's leftovers. Nothing was ever wasted. The Canary Islands archipelago was once at the crossroads of international trade and influences from other parts of the world are still to be found in the *cocina canaria*. Yams from Africa, sweet potatoes from South America and saffron from La Mancha appear in everyday dishes.

MEAT, FISH & *PAPAS*

Meat and fish used to be served only on special occasions. Goats were precious, as they supplied milk. The Canarian sun has always limited food storage times, so the Spanish settlers preserved their food by pickling it in sea salt and marinating it in a spicy concoction known as *adobo*, in which fish and meat did not spoil. These typically Canarian sauces made from oil, vinegar, bay leaves, herbs and garlic are still regarded as the icing on the

cake of the island's cuisine. Just so you know, sea salt from the Salinas de Janubio is a welcome addition to almost any dish.

INSIDER TIP
Flor de sal is where it's at

Small but nippy fishing boats cast their nets into the waters off Lanzarote's coast and haul out *cherne*, *bocinegro* and *vieja*. All are species peculiar to the Canary Islands and every day they quickly make it still fresh into the island's kitchens. *Tuna and sardines* are always worth recommending. Usually they are served simply *a la plancha*, after sizzling in hot oil on a metal skillet. The same is true of seafood. *Choco* (squid) and *pulpo* (octopus) are snacks served with fresh white bread and eaten between meals. Fish and meat are served with *papas arrugadas* and *mojo*, boiled "wrinkled" potatoes in a spicy sauce. They are cooked in brine

Taste some island wine

and eaten with the skin on. Meat is served with *mojo rojo*, a "red sauce" made from chillies, oil, garlic, vinegar and salt, while fish is served with *mojo verde*, a "green sauce" that replaces the chilli with copious amounts of coriander.

FOR IN BETWEEN: TAPAS

Tapas come from the Spanish mainland. These popular "lite bites" have now found their way into the simple bars and cafeterias, where *Lanzaroteños* have breakfast and lunch. In the morning, it is usually enough just to order a *café solo* or a *cortado*, a small black aromatic coffee served with or without milk, plus a *bocadillo* (a large roll with a filling). At lunchtime, i.e. from 1pm, it is the custom to sit at the bar by the display of tapas and snack on a little bowl of

albóndigas (meatballs in sauce), *boquerones* (anchovies) – eaten deep-fried or *en vinagre* (in vinegar) – or any other small delicacies on offer. In the evenings Lanzaroteños spend time with their families. The evening meal eaten en familia does not usually begin until about 10pm. Supper usually consists of something light, which might include tapas, salad and white bread, occasionally fish or *potaje*.

VOLCANIC WINES & BEER

Many families treat themselves at the weekend. After a day on the beach comes a meal in a restaurant, including the luxury of a dessert, perhaps accompanied by a bottle of wine. Lanzarote is – after Tenerife – the largest wine producer in the Canarian archipelago. In recent years, many family-owned cellars have been modernised and new bodegas have opened. At the same time, the quality of the product has improved dramatically and the wines frequently win international prizes. Along La Geria wine route, many bodegas open for wine tastings and visitors are also invited to take tours through the cellars. *Lanzaroteños* also love their beer. There are Canarian brands such as *Dorada* and *Tropical* as well as good *unfiltered beers* from Lanzarote such as *Nao* and *Cervezas Malpaís*. A large bottle of mineral water from Gran Canaria or Tenerife is an essential accompaniment to every meal. A good wayt to see out the evening is with a bottle of local, earthy La Geria wine and a *carajillo*, a strong espresso with a shot of brandy.

Today's Specials

Starters

CALDO DE PESCADO
Fish soup with potatoes and herbs

GAMBAS AL AJILLO
Prawns deep fried in olive oil with garlic and chillies

RANCHO CANARIO
Hearty stew made from chickpeas, pasta, meat and chorizo

Mains

CHERNE AL CILANTRO
Canarian gilthead bream in coriander sauce

SANCOCHO CANARIO
Boiled, salted fish with vegetables and sweet potatoes

CONEJO AL SALMOREJO
Marinaded rabbit

CARNE DE CABRA EN ADOBO
Goat in spicy sauce

Sides

MOJO ROJO
Spicy, red sauce made from chillies, oil, garlic, vinegar and salt

MOJO VERDE
Green sauce with fresh coriander

PAPAS ARRUGADAS
'wrinkled potatoes' (with mojo rojo or verde)

PATATAS FRITAS
chips

GOFIO ESCALDADO
Toasted cereal flour thickened with fish stock to make a porridge

Desserts

LECHE ASADA
"Grilled milk" pudding made from eggs, lemon peel, cinnamon and sugar

BIENMESABE
Sticky, golden-brown dessert made from honey, slivers of almond, egg yolk and lemon. The name translates as "tastes good to me"

FLAN CASERO
Homemade caramel custard

SHOPPING

SHOP TILL YOU DROP

Lanzarote's local markets are a feast for the eyes, especially the Sunday market in Teguise. This little town is transformed into a bazaar of curiosities and kitsch, crafts and culinary delights. The vendor is usually the producer as well: an elderly *señor* selling hand-crafted cane baskets or an ageing hippie behind a table with lava jewellery. The market in Teguise proved to be so successful that many more *mercadillos* (mini-markets) have since appeared on the scene: in Costa Teguise on a Friday evening, in Arrecife, Haría and Playa Blanca on Saturday morning.

A BARGAIN! 🐷

The local people are more likely to do their shopping in Playa Honda, a suburb of Arrecife. Here, functional and well-stocked warehouse and outlet stores line the LZ-2 highway and you will find pretty well everything you are familiar with at home – and with a little luck it might even be cheaper.

FOODIE SOUVENIRS

Lanzarote's wine is available in all supermarkets, but it's best to purchase directly from the bodega. Please note that the local wines are not suitable for storing. One unusual and original product is sea salt from the Salinas de Janubio. It is sold in small, decorative packs. For the best quality, choose the top layer of salt called *flor de sal*, or salt flower. Goat's cheese is just as much a delicacy as the hot and spicy *mojo* sauces. The latter are sold in preserving jars. The sweet dessert known as *bienmesabe* is sold in similar glass jars. All these souvenirs can be bought in supermarkets, as can *ron con miel*. This honey rum is another Canarian speciality, although most of it comes from the neighbouring island of Gran Canaria.

Potter around the Sunday market in Teguise (left); ceramic pictures (right)

POTTERY TRINKETS

Pottery is produced in the traditional way without a potter's wheel. The clay must first be worked into manageable lengths. The potter then lays the pieces on top of each other and rolls them out, smoothing out any uneven-ness with a sharp stone. The bowls and jugs have a natural russet colour. Clay is also used to make the *Novios de El Mojón* (Couple of El Mojón): male and female fertility figurines in early Canarian style with oversized genitals. These are traditionally given to newlyweds as a symbol of a fruitful marriage. Today, of course, the tradition is considered more of a humorous gesture.

ART

Lanzarote is very lucky to have César Manrique, the best-known painter, sculptor and architect in the Canary Islands and a mastermind who continues to inspire and shape the art world to this day. An international community of artists has established itself on the island and their studios are to be found in a number of places, including Arrecife, Yaiza and Teguise.

BORN IN HELL

Often found on the black lava beaches on the west coast are the small, green, shimmering pebbles of olivine. The mineral was hurled upwards from the bowels of the earth together with the magma and later washed out of the clinker by the sea. Pieces of lava studded with olivine are sold as souvenirs for just a couple of euros. Many other shops sell jewellery using this pretty semi-precious stone. However, most of the olivine comes, not from the island, but from South America and Asia, as the fragments found on Lanzarote are usually too small.

SPORT & ACTIVITIES

Because a constant wind is pretty well guaranteed, windsurfing is the number one sport on Lanzarote. Paragliding and hang-gliding are popular too. Diving schools run courses and organise dives at interesting locations such as the Museo Atlántico de Lanzarote off the coast at Playa Blanca. Lanzarote is also a great destination for cyclists and hikers. The guided walks in the Timanfaya National Park leave a lasting impression.

And then there are the special events, including (usually from May to December) beach volleyball tournaments, cycle races and marathon running. One competition that attracts international attention is *Ironman Lanzarote (ironmanlanzarote.com)*, co-organised by the La Santa Sports Hotel, where athletes have to swim 3.8km, cycle 180km round the island and finally run a marathon. The last leg of the course runs from Puerto del Carmen to Arrecife – why not come and congratulate the iron athletes at the finishing line?

CYCLING

The weather on Lanzarote is perfect year-round for all two-wheel enthusiasts. You can safely leave your waterproof clothing at home. Much more important is a plentiful supply of sunblock and a pair of sunglasses. The magnificent volcanic landscape north of Costa Teguise is ideal for mountain bikers. But it is strictly forbidden to leave the (very good) trails. Racing cyclists and tourers will find near-perfect conditions throughout the island. No mountains are higher than 600m, limiting the challenge. Cyclists will discover countless natural phenomena and scenic attractions on their travels, for example along the southeast coast.

The wild conditions at Playa de Famara are perfect for kitesurfing

Addresses to note for cyclists are: Playa Blanca: *Cool Bikes (mountain bikes from 16 euros/day; e-bikes and scooters | C/ El Correíllo 48 | tel. 928 51 77 87 | coolbikes.es)*

Costa Teguise: *Tommy's Bike Station (mountain bike 16–25 euros/day | Av. Islas Canarias 12 | CC Las Maretas 20B | to the right of the post office | mobile tel. 628 10 21 77 | tommys-bikes.com)* hires out excellent mountain bikes and offers free delivery of bikes to your holiday hotel.

Puerto del Carmen: *Renner Bikes (mountain bikes from 12 euros/day, racing bikes from 19 euros/day | CC Marítimo 25 Alto | tel. 928 51 06 12 | mountainbike-lanzarote.com)*.

DIVING

The underwater fauna off the Canary Islands is interesting and varied. One of the most memorable dives is off the coast near La Mala. Countless stingrays and eagle rays live on the seabed in the clear water. All diving schools request a one-off contribution of around 15 euros for the decompression chamber in Arrecife.

Costa Teguise: The *Aquatis Diving Centre Lanzarote (dive 30 euros, with equipment 40 euros | Playa de las Cucharas, Local 6 | tel. 928 59 04 07 | diving-lanzarote.net)* offers dives and lessons (also to children).

Playa Blanca: Many courses and dives on offer at *Rubicon Diving (10 dives 420 euros | Marina Rubicón | Local 77b | tel. 928 34 93 46 | rubicondiving.com)*.

Puerto del Carmen: The Playa de la Barilla near the old harbour is the starting point for many dives. One popular underwater attraction is the *Catedral*, a 20m lava bubble in a vertical wall. A number of providers lead close to it, including *Safari Diving (dive with complete equipment 39 euros, 10 dives 337 euros | Playa de la Barrilla 4 | tel. 928 51 19 92 | www.safaridiving.com);* and *Island Watersports (dives from 30 euros, 10 dives 246 euros | Av. del Varadero 36 | Marina | tel. 928 51 18 80 | dive lanzarote.com).*

GOLF

A semidesert with lush carpets of green grass behind an ocean of blue: Lanzarote's golf courses are breathtakingly beautiful. The 18-hole course of *Golf Costa Teguise (daily 8am–8pm | green-fee 70 euros | tel. 928 59 05 12 | lanzarote-golf.com)* boasts a long tradition. Also attractive is the newer 18-hole course at *Lanzarote Golf (daily 8am–8pm | green-fee 75 euros | access via LZ-505 | tel. 928 51 40 50 | lanzarotegolfresort.com),* near Puerto del Carmen.

HANG-GLIDING

The preferred launch-pad for hang-gliders is the 502m Montaña Tinasoria near Puerto del Carmen. Lift-offs are also possible from various points on the Risco de Famara and near Mala. But take care: the thermals on Lanzarote can be very strong, and unpredictable changes in wind direction are frequent. There have already been many serious accidents, so beginners should only take off under expert supervision. Find experts at *volcanofly-lanzarote.com* and *lanzarote-tandemflights.com.*

HIKING

Lanzarote might not be a green hiker's paradise, but there are some marked trails. The *Camino Natural de Órzola a Playa Blanca* crosses the island from north to south. Hiking tours around the Fire Mountains are also

spectacular, organised, for example, by *Lanzatrekk (lanzatrekk.com)*.

STAND-UP PADDLE BOARDING

Ever given it a go? SUP is offered in all the resort areas. You can rent the necessary equipment and take lessons in Costa Teguise at *SUP Lanzarote (Playa de los Charcos | suplanzarote. com)*; in Puerto del Carmen at *Lava Flow Surf (lavaflowsurf.com);* and in Playa Blanca at *Kaboti Surf (kabotisurf. com)*.

SURFING

Experienced surfers with short boards reckon the conditions off Playa de Famara – which sees high, long-breaking waves – rank among the best on the island. But caution is advised as there are some dangerous currents in these parts. *Costa Noroeste (course from 35 euros/half day | Av. El Marinero 11 | La Caleta de Famara | tel. 928 52 85 97 | costanoroeste.com)*.

Windsurfing addicts also get their money's worth in the stormy waters of La Caleta de Farmara. But the classic wind- and kitesurfing spot is Costa Teguise, to the island's east. Strong side winds blow on the Playa de las Cucharas. International windsurfing competitions are regularly staged here.

Windsurf Paradise (C/ la Corvina 8 | tel. 635 05 41 10 | windsurf lanzarote.com) and the *Windsurfing Club* (see p. 53) offer very good facilities including board rental. Boards cost from 40 euros per day to hire, beginners' courses from 90 euros.

At *Calima Surf (Av. El Marinero 13 | tel. 928 52 85 28 | calimasurf.com)* in La Caleta de Famara, watersports services on offer include the loan of boards, and windsurfing, surfing and kitesurfing lessons.

Clear your head on a walk through the island's barren landscape

REGIONAL OVERVIEW

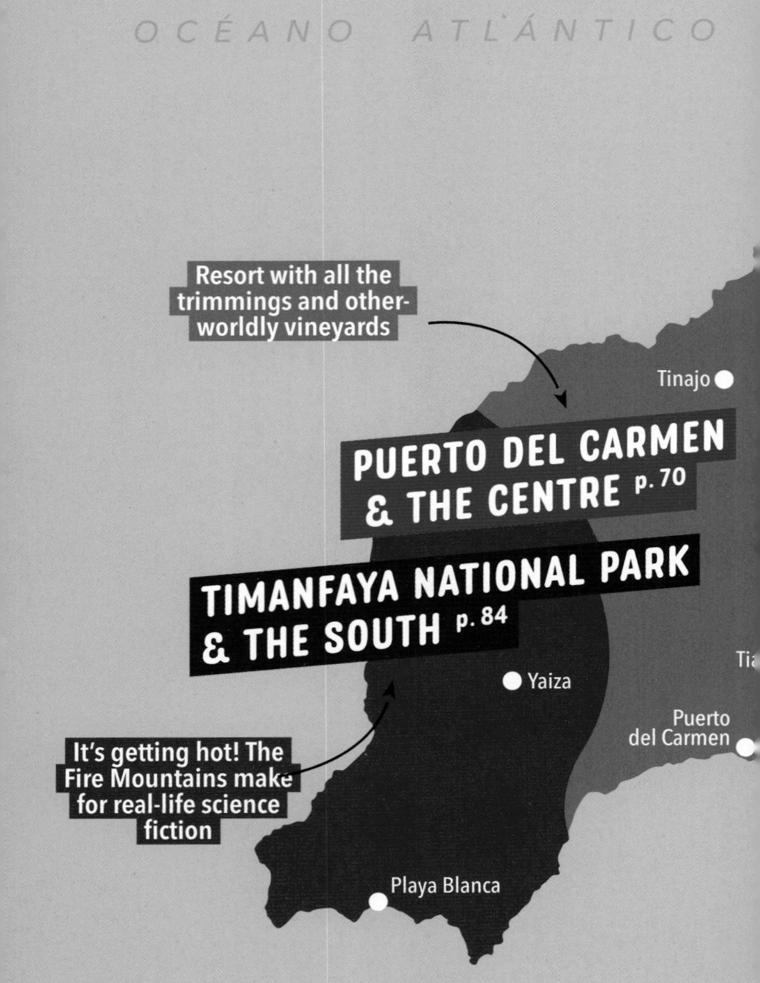

OCÉANO ATLÁNTICO

Resort with all the trimmings and other-worldly vineyards

Tinajo ●

PUERTO DEL CARMEN & THE CENTRE p. 70

TIMANFAYA NATIONAL PARK & THE SOUTH p. 84

● Yaiza

Ti

Puerto del Carmen ●

It's getting hot! The Fire Mountains make for real-life science fiction

Playa Blanca ●

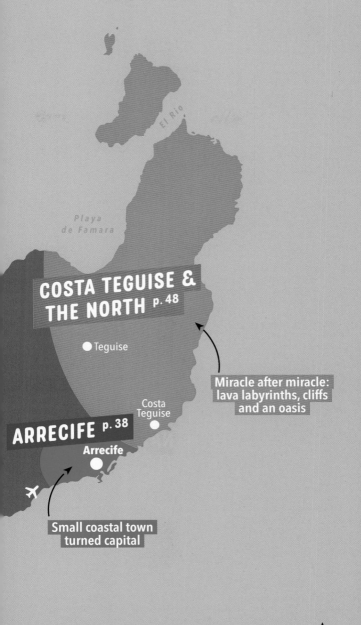

El Río

Playa
de Famara

COSTA TEGUISE &
THE NORTH p. 48

● Teguise

Costa
Teguise
●

Miracle after miracle:
lava labyrinths, cliffs
and an oasis

ARRECIFE p. 38

Arrecife ●

Small coastal town
turned capital

5 km
3.11 mi

ARRECIFE

A CITY IN SEARCH OF A FACELIFT

Located on the coastline with reefs that jut far out to sea, Arrecife is like something from a dream. The island's capital has a great beach with light-coloured sand and swaying palms, plus an atmospheric lagoon and marina.

As you get further inland, however, the magic starts to fade. Dingy streets, shops shuttered since the crisis, a deserted party strip and odd gaps between buildings – the capital's in a bit of a sorry state. You get the impression that the money that flowed in during the

Arrecife's old town, with the Iglesia de Ginés, makes a good first impression

tourist boom passed by the capital. That said, an ambitious facelift has begun, starting with the coastline and the parallel traffic-controlled street complete with wide promenade. The road goes down to the marina, where jetties lead out onto the water and sleek boats rest at anchor to create the city's showpiece.

Just as nice for a stroll or simply to relax is the Charco de San Ginés, a seawater lagoon where little fishing boats bob up and down on the water.

ARRECIFE

MARCO POLO HIGHLIGHTS

★ EL CHARCO DE SAN GINÉS

This attractively renovated natural harbour is being transformed into a lively bar and restaurant quarter, surrounded by a pedestrian zone ➤ p. 43

★ MARINA LANZAROTE

Wrested back from the sea is this marina, which offers shops and restaurants. The perfect spot to relax ➤ p. 44

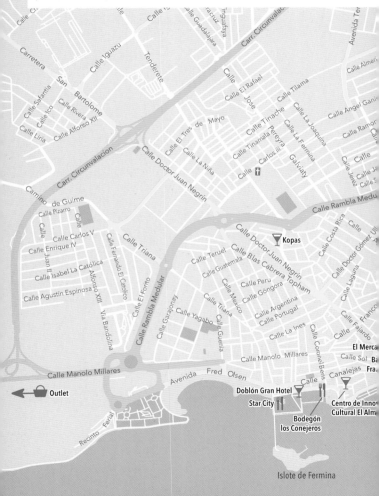

★ **CASTILLO DE SAN JOSÉ**
The squat castle surprises with the admirable Museum of Contemporary Art and a stylish restaurant ➤ p. 44

Carr. Circunvalación

Calle Oceano · Glaciar Ártico

Calle Oceano · Índico

Carretera de los Marmoles

Castillos

Calle Teléstoro Bra…

Calle León y Castillo

Calle Vizcaya

Castillo de San José ★ 6 ¶¶ QuéMUAC Castillo de San José

Calle Muelle de los Marmoles

Calle Palencia

Carretera de los

Calle Escatilla

Calle Velacho

Avenida de Naos

Calle Rambla Medular

Velázquez

Galdós · Calle Cáceres

Islota de las Cruces

Lérida

Calle Pérez

Calle Extremadura

Calle La Añaza

Avenida De Naos

4 **Marina Lanzarote ★**

Calle La Palma

to Borges · Díaz

Palme

Lilium ¶¶

Calle Las Golondrinas

2 **El Charco de San Ginés ★**

Market Ave. Olof

Pescadería Municipal & La Recova

Iglesia de San Ginés

Strava

Islote del Francés

OCÉANO

Municipal

astillo de San Gabriel

le San Gabriel

ATLÁNTICO

↑
400 m
437 yd

Arrecife is no beauty, but it does have a few quite attractive places, such as the lagoon with its neighbouring marina and a beach that is protected by reefs. If you are curious to know more about life in one of the Canary Islands' capital cities, then this is the place to come.

The eye-catcher on the seafront is the Gran Hotel, Lanzarote's only high-rise block. It's safe to say landscape architect César Manrique was less than amused when he first saw the 17-storey block in the 1970s. Today, sporting a chic glass façade, the hotel has been extensively restyled to give it a new lease of life. At the foot of the hotel is the Playa del Reducto, a dreamy beach studded with palm trees. The southern end, the beach

merges into a park, meaning the relaxation zone – now signposted in green – carries on a little further. Once on the promenade, you can keep going! If it takes your fancy, try walking the 10km along the seafront to Puerto del Carmen. The other side of the Gran Hotel is also looking good: walk along the traffic-controlled coastal road dotted with terraced cafés to the beautiful ☛ *Casa de Cultura Agustín de la Hoz*, and check out their latest exhibition. Behind it, you can cross the Puente de Bolas drawbridge onto an embankment that juts far into the sea. Halfway down is the Castillo de San Gabriel with its impressive interior. Inland, Calle León y Castillo is an inviting spot for a stroll. This pedestrianised zone with its narrow alleyways takes you deep into the vibrant heart of urban Arrecife. Businessmen, mothers with children, casually dressed *señoritas* and Canarian *señores* with their typical wide-brimmed hats go about their day on these streets. Make sure to come early because the streets empty when it's siesta time shortly after 1pm. To the right, the church tower of Iglesia de San Ginés rises up between the maze of houses. With its benches and shady laurel trees, the small plaza in front of the simple church is the perfect place to sit down and take a break.

The jewel in Arrecife's crown lies in the quarter behind the church and the market: the Charco de San Ginés, the small natural harbour or "pond" *(charco)*. It is fun to walk round the promenade lining its shores. And don't worry about getting tired

WHERE TO START?

Seaside promenade: The best place to start a stroll through Lanzarote's capital is the seaside promenade. Park your car nearby (e.g. in the underground car park of the Arrecife Gran Hotel); the town is quite small, but the congestion can be frustrating. If you are arriving by bus, get off at the promenade, too. Walk about 500m along the beach until you come to the Casa de Cultura Agustín de la Hoz, a magnificently restored building with tourist information. Head inland to where the León y Castillo pedestrianised street branches off, which is close to the Charco de San Ginés, the town's lagoon.

Daily life is unhurried on Calle León y Castillo

– there's a terrace bar where you can take a break pretty much every three steps. Down by the lagoon, a piece of land has been reclaimed from the sea, and footbridges stretch across the new marina. A bit further away from the centre, near the ferry docks and the cruise port, the Castillo de San José sits up on a cliff. As in days past, it still marks Arrecife's city limits.

SIGHTSEEING

1 CASTILLO DE SAN GABRIEL

This little construction with a few measly canons on its roof is supposed to be a fortress? The pirates certainly didn't seem overly impressed by it as they regularly dropped anchor at Lanzarote, looted villages and took hostages. The site chosen for the fortress in 1590 is also rather odd: it perches on an island just off the coast

that is connected to the city by means of a drawbridge. The dyke continues just beyond the fort so that it is possible to walk quite a distance "on the water". A museum inside the fortress depicts the island's history from the original indigenous inhabitants to the Spanish conquest and to the present-day tourism boom. Climb the narrow stone steps to the "upper deck" to enjoy the impressive view of Arrecife's coast. *Mon–Fri 10am–5pm, Sat 10am–2pm | admission 3 euros (accompanying text guide available) | ⏱ 30 mins.*

2 EL CHARCO DE SAN GINÉS ★

The harbour in the centre of Arrecife is a fine example of how to redevelop a run-down urban area. Bobbing up and down on the shallow water are brightly coloured fishing boats, which blend in with the striking blue and white houses and create a pretty overall impression. A promenade leads around the harbour. Restaurants set out tables along it when the weather is good. Snack on a tapa and relax while watching the fishing boats enter and exit by a canal.

3 IGLESIA DE SAN GINÉS

The white, three-naved basilica blends in well with the small, tree-lined Plaza de las Palmas. In the cool interior, the beautiful wooden ceiling in *mudéjar* style, the black columns of lava stone and the stone circular arches supporting the roof beams create a warm atmosphere. *No fixed opening times*

4 MARINA LANZAROTE ★

The modern marina with trendy shops and casual dining options has become the jewel in Arrecife's crown. Bright, cubic architecture, plus sleek yachts on long piers – many see the marina as a stroke of architectural genius. *ccmarinalanzarote.com*

5 PARQUE MUNICIPAL

West of the town beach, the extended promenade opens out into a small park full of exotic plants. Children can let off steam here at a playground with a skating park. The buses from Playa Blanca, Puerto del Carmen and Costa Teguise stop on the northern side of the park. This small bus terminal *(intercambiador de guaguas)* is worth noting, as the footpath to the town centre, which starts here, is a much shorter route than the one from the central bus station.

6 CASTILLO DE SAN JOSÉ ★ ☂

Almost 200 years had to go by before the Spanish king came to the realization that a second fort would be necessary. It was built above the fishing harbour along the coast road to Costa Teguise and looks remarkably like the first one. Inside, however, a completely different world unfolds: the *Museo Internacional de Arte Contemporáneo (MIAC), (daily 10am–8pm | admission 4 euros | cact-lanzarote.com).* The list of artists in this Museum of Contemporary Art reads like a Who's Who of Spanish modern art: Joan Miró, Antoni Tàpies and Pablo Picasso, to name but three. One room is dedicated to Pancho Lasso (1904–73), one of Lanzarote's most celebrated 20th-century sculptors. Thanks to César Manrique, the architecture of the Castillo has been given a nudge towards the modern age: a stunning staircase built into a white tunnel leads down to the *restaurant* (see below) on the lower level, where panoramic windows spanning the length of the room look out over the harbour. Make sure you also pay a visit to the viewing platform. ⏲ *60 mins.*

EATING & DRINKING

BAR SAN FRANCISCO 🐖

It has not really kept up with the times, but Bar San Francisco is still a hotspot. The brightly tiled restaurant bar is always busy, from the first *café cortado* in the morning until the last glass of wine in the evening. Wide selection of tapas. *Closed Sun | C/ León y Castillo 10–12 | tel. 928 81 33 83 | €*

Works of art by Miró, Picasso and others can be found inside the Castillo de San José

BODEGÓN LOS CONEJEROS

Reached via a narrow alleyway, this rustic-style restaurant serves authentic Lanzarote cuisine to a discerning clientele. *Mon–Sat 6pm–midnight | Av. Dr Rafael González 9 | tel. 928 18 71 95 | €€*

LILIUM

Great cuisine at the new marina: Orlando cooks creative island dishes from local ingredients while Sandra serves. The nine-course tasting menu for €45 offers seasonal delights – from banana croquettes to pork cheeks on sweet potato and home-made goat's milk ice cream. *Mon–Sat 2–4pm and 8–11pm | Av.*

INSIDER TIP
The easy choice

Olof Palme | Marina | tel. 928 52 49 78 | restaurantelilium.com | €€

QUÉMUAC CASTILLO DE SAN JOSÉ

Dine out in a castle! The entrance of black lava steps and subtly illuminated walls looks inviting. Panoramic windows reveal a great view over the harbour, while sophisticated waiters serve modern Canarian cuisine with pizzazz and just a touch of luxury. If you don't want to eat, just savour the atmosphere at the bar. *Daily | tel. 928 81 23 21 | €– €€€*

STAR CITY

Up in the air! The pub/café on the 17th floor of the Arrecife Gran Hotel can boast not just a superb selection of

The empty loungers soon fill up once the sun goes down

drinks, but also a fine view over the island's capital. *Daily | Parque Islas Canarias | aghotelspa.com | €*

STRAVA

This dedicated mini locale on a side street off the church square offers a different selection of mouth-watering tapas every day, including octopus on chickpea mash, tuna tartare and calamari croquettes. *C/ Ginés de Castro 9-B | tel. 928 80 63 94 | €–€€*

SHOPPING

The pedestrian-friendly Calle León y Castillo and its side streets form the main shopping area. Modern retailers share the sidewalks with traditional shops.

EL MERCADILLO

Nicely antiquated: small retail centre with shops around a glass-covered patio – including an organic food shop *(herbolario)* and a friendly café. *C/ León y Castillo 16*

MARKET

On Saturday morning, market stalls in the narrow lanes around the church sell arts and crafts and food. *Sat 9am–noon | Plaza de las Palmas*

OUTLET

The outlet and shopping centres in Playa Honda, a suburb 2km south of the capital, sell absolutely everything – and the prices aren't half bad! The *Centro Comercial Deiland* sells branded goods at bargain prices and

trees. The waves break on offshore reefs, allowing for worry-free bathing.

NIGHTLIFE

CENTRO DE INNOVACIÓN CULTURAL EL ALMACÉN

The island's cultural hub: there is something going on almost every evening – concerts, cinema, theatre, performance or art exhibitions. Follow it up with a drink at the bar... El Almacén has been setting the scene for decades. *Closed Sun | C/ José Betancort 33 | culturaalanzarote.com*

DOBLÓN GRAN HOTEL

At the Gran Hotel Arrecife: DJs keep the party going until dawn at the "Doubloon". *Daily 11pm–6am | Av. de Mancomunidad 1 | FB: doblon gran hotel*

INSIDER TIP
Well-stocked

is where many *Lanzaroteños* go to shop. The Hiperdino supermarket has the largest selection of groceries on the island.

PESCADERÍA MUNICIPAL & LA RECOVA

For self-caterers: fresh foods are sold at the small fish market and adjacent walled-in market patio. *Mon–Sat 8am–1pm | corner C/ Liebre/Av. Vargas*

BEACHES

PLAYA DEL REDUCTO

Treat yourself to some downtime on Arrecife's prime beach! It has soft white sand and is shaded by palm

WHERE TO STAY IN ARRECIFE

SEA VIEWS & A CASTLE

The name *Miramar (85 rooms | Av. Coll 2 | tel. 928 81 26 00 | hmiramar.com | €€)* pretty much says it all: you can enjoy the *mira mar* (sea view) both from the balconies of the charming rooms as well as from the breakfast terrace. And the hotel is directly opposite the Castillo de San Gabriel and its drawbridge: just cross the traffic-controlled street and walk down the rocky steps and you're in the Atlantic!

COSTA TEGUISE & THE NORTH

ONE SURPRISE AFTER THE NEXT

Exploring the north from the holiday town of Costa Teguise, you will encounter the many sides of Lanzarote – from the desert to the valley of palms, from dusty plains to the dramatic Famara mountain range, with several highlights on the way.

Lanzarote reaches heights of 671m in the north, high enough for the trade wind clouds to trigger vital rainfall. This makes for a lot of green, as in the oasis-like valley of Haría, with its Canarian palms. Similarly, the cliffs to the west are dotted with green, while grapevines

The now dormant Monte Corona volcano is responsible for the north's dramatic landscapes

creep along the slopes of Monte Corona. A volcanic eruption in 3000 BCE created two amazing cave systems that can be visited today: the Jameos del Agua and the Cueva de los Verdes. Above them, the sombre lunar landscape of sharp-edged magma clumps stretches eastward to the coast. Despite the darkness, there are many beaches of fine golden sand on this part of the coast. Finally, you reach the fishing village of Órzola, renowned for its good fish restaurants. Mini ferries to the remote island of La Graciosa leave from here.

COSTA TEGUISE & THE NORTH

MARCO POLO HIGHLIGHTS

★ **FUNDACIÓN CÉSAR MANRIQUE**
Manrique's home in a lava bubble in Tahiche brings art and nature into harmony ➤ p. 54

★ **JARDÍN DE CACTUS**
It's a fascinating sight: the spiky world of 1,400 cacti with a windmill and fishpond ➤ p. 55

★ **JAMEOS DEL AGUA**
The mysterious lagoon with white crabs is the main attraction of the lava tunnel ➤ p. 56

★ **CUEVA DE LOS VERDES**
A visit to the magnificent cave system is a highlight of every holiday on Lanzarote ➤ p. 57

★ **LA GRACIOSA**
This remote, unspoilt island has retained much of its original charm ➤ p. 58

★ **TEGUISE**
A one-off combination of church, palaces and townhouses in the former capital ➤ p. 60

★ **HARÍA**
For many, this is the prettiest place on the island, nestling in a valley among a thousand palm trees ➤ p. 67

★ **MIRADOR DEL RÍO**
The islands of La Graciosa and Alegranza are visible from one of Lanzarote's finest viewpoints ➤ p. 69

Lanzarote

La Caleta de Fa

La Santa

Sóo

12km, 15 mins

Muñique

Tinajo

Tiagua

Mancha Blanca

ESPAÑA (CANARIAS)

Mozaga

El Islote

La Florida

San Bartolomé

Masdache

Montaña Blanca

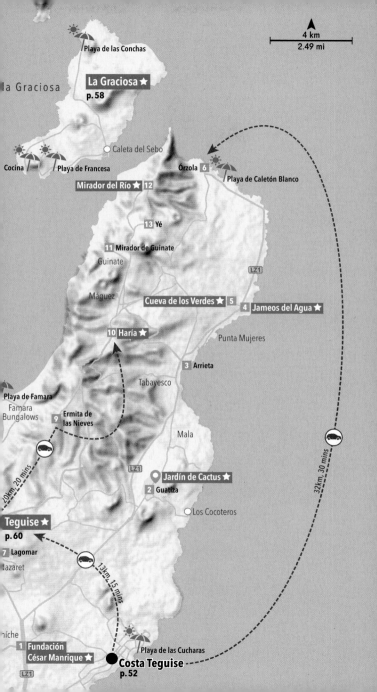

Playa de las Conchas

La Graciosa ★
p. 58

la Graciosa

Caleta del Sebo

Cocina   Playa de Francesa

Órzola **6**

Playa de Caletón Blanco

Mirador del Río ★ 12

13 Yé

11 Mirador de Guinate

Guinate

LZ1

Máguez

Cueva de los Verdes ★ 5   **4 Jameos del Agua ★**

10 Haría ★

Punta Mujeres

Playa de Famara
Famara
Bungalows

9 Ermita de
las Nieves

3 Arrieta

Tabayesco

Mala

20km 20 mins

LZ1

Jardín de Cactus ★

2 Guatiza

Los Cocoteros

32km 30 mins

Teguise ★
p. 60

7 Lagomar

Nazaret

13km 15 mins

Playa de las Cucharas

1 Fundación
César Manrique ★

● **Costa Teguise**
p. 52

LZ1

4 km
2.49 mi

Costa Teguise: dark mountains, white houses and watersports

COSTA TEGUISE

(□□ G9) **Anyone who is just looking to relax a little on the beach has come to the right place at Costa Teguise. There are a couple of lovely, small beaches with a promenade, a few windsurfing and diving schools as well as nice restaurants.**

The developed plots of land that extend deep inland clearly show the size of the original tourism expansion plans. But since the economic crisis (2008–16), calm has returned due to lack of funds and the authorities in Teguise are now pursuing a more leisurely development plan. As a result, the holiday experience in the tourist village north of the island's capital is gentler than in lively Puerto del Carmen. Despite that, some hotels here are reckoned to be the best in the Canaries, the five-star Gran Meliá Salinas being a fine example.

SIGHTSEEING

PUEBLO MARINERO

The "mariners' village" bears the unmistakeable signature of César Manrique, as winding courtyards replace the historic town centre. It's also home to the large weekly market and the main carnival celebration in February. *Av. de las Islas Canarias s/n*

LANZAROTE AQUARIUM 🐠 🕴

About 20 well-illuminated tanks recreate the habitats of many sea creatures, and sharks swim in a glass tunnel above the visitors. *Daily 10am–6pm |*

52

admission 14 euros, children 9 euros | Av. Las Acacias | Centro Comercial El Trébol | aquariumlanzarote.com | ⏱ 45 mins

EATING & DRINKING

The trade winds that blow along Costa Teguise's coastal strip used to be a source of irritation for restaurant waiters. Much of their time was spent chasing flying tablecloths. To prevent this many restaurant terraces today are either protected from the wind or glazed with panoramic screens, so that waiting staff can get on with their work – and diners don't have to keep removing sand from their food and teeth.

CEBOLLA SALVAJE

You'll get a little more than the "Estudio Bar" promised in the understatement of the century: José and Elena serve Canarian-inspired tapas and dishes made using regional ingredients, accompanied by natural, unpasteurised beer from Lanzarote brand Malpaís. The cocktails are delicious too! Daily | C/ Las Olas 21 | tel. 928 59 07 07 | FB: cebolla salvaje | €€

SIDER TIP
Craft beer & craft food

LA TABLA

An airy terrace (though not directly by the sea) awaits at this eatery. Sit back on your padded chair and enjoy the friendly service and affordable tapas menu, with seven small dishes guaranteed to satisfy two people. If you are really hungry, then try the charcoal-grilled meat dishes. The home-made desserts are also tasty. Daily | Centro Comercial Las Maretas | near the post office | tel. 928 52 40 76 | €–€€

VALI 🐷

This pavilion at the bottom of the avenue leading down to the beach at Costa Teguise is the perfect place to fill up on sandwiches, smoothies and a strong coffee for just a few euros. Tue–Sun 9.30am–1pm | Av. del Jablillo s/n/ Ap. Galeón | €

VILLA TOLEDO

Restaurant with terrace right on the seafront above rocks – perfect at sunset. Large fish and meat menu. Daily | Av. Los Cocederos | tel. 928 59 06 26 | €€

SHOPPING

MERCADILLO

The Pueblo Marinero is the atmospheric backdrop to the Friday evening market (from 5pm). Artisans from all over the island sell lava jewellery and watercolours with Lanzarote motifs, fabrics and pottery.

SPORT & ACTIVITIES

AQUATIS DIVING CENTER

This diving school organises everything from beginner to professional courses, including night and wreck diving. Playa de las Cucharas, Local 6 | tel. 928 59 04 07 | diving-lanzarote.net

TOMMY'S BIKE STATION

Fulfil all your cycling desires here with racing, mountain and e-bikes plus guided tours all around the island. *Av. Islas Canarias 12 | CC Las Maretas 20-B | tel. 628 10 21 77 | tommys-bikes. com*

WINDSURFING CLUB

The venerable shop offers windsurfing and SUP courses, snorkelling and kayak excursions. *C/ Marajo | CC Las Maretas 2 | tel. 928 59 07 31 | lanzarotewindsurf.com*

BEACHES

Good things come in small packages, and these ones have light, powdery sand. At 650m, the longest beach here is 🏖 *Playa de las Cucharas*, which is also popular with surfers. *Playa del Jablillo* and *Playa Bastián*, shaded by palm trees, are great spots to the south. Then there's *Playa del Ancla* below the Hotel Oasis de Lanzarote. All beaches can be reached via the promenade.

NIGHTLIFE

Only at the weekend do the clubs and bars in the Pueblo Marinero fill up. The nightlife is aimed primarily at British tourists. *Dicken's Bar (daily until 2.30am | Av. del Mar)* may sound Victorian, but it belongs to a Spaniard named Víctor who mixes good cocktails and stocks a large selection of gins, including Canarian Macaronesian; live music several times a week.

AROUND COSTA TEGUISE

1 FUNDACIÓN CÉSAR MANRIQUE ★ ☂

7km west of Costa Teguise / 5 mins by car via the LZ 34

Visitors to Lanzarote keen on gaining a better understanding of the island's greatest artist will almost certainly want to pay a visit to the Fundación César Manrique in *Tahiche*. The foundation occupies the artist's former home, which is situated near a roundabout showcasing a large Manrique mobile made from stainless steel. A large part of César Manrique's oeuvre and also pieces by his artist friends are exhibited here, but the extraordinary house alone is worth a visit: one remarkable feature is the futuristic underground lounge built into lava bubbles. *Daily 10am–6pm | admission 8 euros | fcmanrique.org | ⏱ 30 mins.*

Another remarkable architectural structure originally designed by Manrique is the nearby restaurant *Los Aljibes de Tahiche (Fri–Wed 11am–10pm | exit the roundabout towards Costa Teguise | mobile tel. 610 45 42 94 | €€–€€€)*, built within a former cistern. A Brazilian-Argentine duo cooks up meat on the grill as well as home-made beer that you can enjoy on the terrace shaded by palms and dragon

INSIDER TIP
Home-brewed beer

trees. Make sure you check out the art gallery in the cistern! *F9*

2 GUATIZA

*11km north of Costa Teguise /
10 mins by car via the LZ 1*

Fields of cacti as far as the eye can see. Every open space in and around Guatiza is planted with the fleshy opuntia cactus. Farmers with low-fitting straw hats pass along the long rows. An avenue of old eucalyptus trees runs through the village, which was once prosperous thanks to the cochineal beetle. Although the trade in natural dyes is now mostly over, between Guatiza and Mala the tiny creatures are still painstakingly harvested.

The ★ *Jardín de Cactus (daily 10am–5.45pm | admission 5.80 euros | ⏱ 30 mins)* at the end of the village is devoted to the prickly world of cacti. César Manrique collected almost 1,500 different types of cactus in the broad pit of a former quarry at the foot of a restored *gofio* mill. The cactus garden was his last creation. Fragments of black lava and high stone columns add to this bizarre setting, so it is not surprising visitors imagine themselves lost in an alien world. A restaurant here serves snacks and a shop sells souvenirs. *G–H7*

3 ARRIETA

*17.5km north of Costa Teguise /
15 mins by car via the LZ 1*

White houses line the oceanfront and a jetty juts out into the water. Every day, fishing boats head out to sea from here to supply the restaurants along the main road with fresh seafood. There is also a beautiful beach in Arrieta: the 800-m-long *Playa de la Garita* may be strewn with rocks, but in between glistens light-coloured sand. For sightseers the only place of interest in the town is the *Casa Juanita*, known as the Blue House or *Casa Azul*. It was built on a cliff by a *Lanzaroteño* who had amassed a fortune in Venezuela. The deep blue upper façade panelling shines from afar. Although it is not a museum in the strict sense of the word, the *Museo de Aloe (closed Sun | C/ El Cortijo 2)* on the edge of town displays all kinds of information about this "miracle plant" on the way to the actual shop.

Stick to the path in the Jardín de Cactus

Wander among the lava funnels, caves and pools at Jameos del Agua

Most visitors come to Arrieta for the fish restaurants. Situated on the pier, equipped with a large ship's telescope and offering a view of the Blue House, is *El Charcón (closed Wed | tel. 928 84 81 10 | elcharconlanzarote. com | €€)*, where Ricardo and Sabina happily dispense the La Grieta house wine.

INSIDER TIP
A delicious red

Their white wine and the rather rare, for Lanzarote, red have designation of origin status and are wonderfully earthy and very drinkable. Always popular is a visit to *Amanecer (closed Thu | La Garita 46 | tel. 928 83 54 84 | €€)*, where a team of brothers cook simple but delicious freshly caught fish. The tables on the small terrace right by the sea fill up quickly. Take a seat at *Chiringo Beach (daily from 11am | $)*, south of town at *Playa de la Garita*, for sandwiches and tapas to the backdrop of cool jazz music. Come at the weekend for delicious seafood paella! *H6*

INSIDER TIP
Perfect paella

▙ JAMEOS DEL AGUA ★
22km north of Costa Teguise / 20 mins by car via the LZ 1

Hollywood actress Rita Hayworth considered them to be the "Eighth Wonder of the World". Even though this may seem a bit exaggerated, the *Jameos del Agua* really are something quite special. First, visitors descend through a wide funnel, a collapsed lava ceiling, and pass a subterranean, terraced restaurant overgrown with lush plants. Still deeper, an enchanting and shimmering saltwater lake is home to a species of white crab that you can't see anywhere else in the world. As the creatures survive in the dark, they have no sight. A sign warns: Do not throw coins into the water, as the metal oxide would poison the crabs.

You climb up to a second cave on the opposite side of the lake. The roof of the cave is open so wide that the sun can penetrate down into the cave, which makes this the perfect spot for a spectacular white pool surrounded by palm trees. In the next lava tube there is an auditorium boasting superb acoustics.

Like the Cueva de los Verdes, the Jameos del Agua is part of the Atlántida tunnel system. Until the late 1960s farmers deposited refuse through two gaping holes *(jameos)* in the lava blanket. A debt of gratitude is owed to César Manrique for clearing out and saving the *jameos* and transforming it into a magical work of natural art. *Daily 10am–6.30pm; Tue, Fri and Sat also 7pm–3am with 45-minute folklore show from 10.30pm, after that DJ sessions until 12.30am | admission 9.50 euros | centrosturisticos.com | ⏱ 30 mins | ◫ H6*

5 CUEVA DE LOS VERDES
★ 🐒 🎏

23km north of Costa Teguise / 20 mins by car via the LZ 1
The perfect journey into the underworld: descend into the bowels of a volcano! As your guide takes you down, you feel as though you are in a giant walk-through sculpture complete with ingenious lighting effects

and spherical sounds. The Cueva de los Verdes is part of a 7.5km lava tunnel, the *Túnel de la Atlántida*. The cave was formed when Monte Corona erupted 5,000 years ago. Streams of lava, which at the time flowed into the sea, quickly cooled down at the surface, while the hot magma beneath continued on its course. When the eruptions stopped, the residues flowed out, leaving behind galleries and caverns at various levels, which together reach a height of 40m and extend far out into the sea. At the time of the pirate attacks the Cueva de los Verdes served as a refuge, as it was well hidden. In 1618, however, Algerian buccaneers discovered the caves through an act of betrayal and carried off the hundreds of people seeking refuge into slavery.

The guided tour (in Spanish and English) through this bizarre underworld inside the lava lasts 45 minutes and covers a distance of 2km. Halfway along there's a large auditorium where everyone can take a rest. At the end, there's another special effect, but we won't spoil the experience by giving away details. Concerts are held in the auditorium – a special experience! *Daily 10am–5pm | admission 9 euros (including guided tour) | centros turisticos.com | ◫ H6*

6 ÓRZOLA

32km north of Costa Teguise / 30 mins by car via the LZ 1
The small fishing port in the far north of the island is definitely worth a visit, if only to watch ferocious Atlantic surf crashing against the rocks. There are a

number of rustic fish restaurants here. The ocean's harvest is served fresh in the *Os Gallegos (daily from 10am | C/ La Quemadita 6 | tel. 928 84 25 02 | €€)*, which has a prime location. Toni swiftly brings out the dishes his wife Begonia has prepared: tender Galician-style (i.e. sliced) octopus, mussels, prawns and overflowing fish platters. But make sure you leave room for the delicious desserts!

INSIDER TIP
Party atmosphere

On weekends, a folk band gets things going with epic love songs! But people don't just come to Órzola to eat. Almost every hour, little boats shuttle between the port and the neighbouring island of La Graciosa.

There are a number of fine beaches nearby. The spectacular *Playa de la Cantería* beneath the towering Famara mountains can be reached as part of a walk. Southeast of Órzola, only a few metres from the LZ 1, there are more magnificent beaches to explore, such as the sandy 🏖 *Caletón Blanco*.

INSIDER TIP
White, whiter, whitest

Note here the striking contrast between the black lava rocks and the almost snow-white sand. Because the water in the sheltered bays is shallow, the sea is several degrees warmer than elsewhere.

If you take the LZ 204 heading to Yé for 2km, you will reach 🐾 *Granja Las Pardelas (daily 10am–6pm | admission 4.50, children 3.50, donkey ride 3.50 euros | La Quemadita 88 | Órzola | pardelas-park.com | ⏱ 60 mins)*, a small petting zoo with goats, rabbits, a

horse and donkeys. Donkey rides are available and, afterwards, children can hone their artistic skills by making pottery. It's also worth stopping a little further on at the aloe vera plantation *Lanzaloe (Mon–Sat 11am–5pm | C/ La Quemadita 96 | lanzaloe.com | ⏱ 20 mins)*. Chemicals are not used here either to grow or process the plants. Try the 🍽 free samples of culinary delicacies as well as cosmetics all made with aloe vera. ▢ H4

LA GRACIOSA

(▢ G3–4) **Anyone wishing to make the crossing from Órzola to the tiny island of ★ La Graciosa needs good sea legs: during the first ten minutes of the journey the small boats are buffeted by the high waves of the untamed Atlantic Ocean.**

But once into the El Río straits the waves usually subside and the waters become much calmer and give way to a wonderful view of the cliffs rising from the sea. This island is a thoroughly agreeable relic from the past. Before the advent of tourism to the Canaries, this is what life was like on the islands – or at least it'll give you an idea. The main village of *Caleta del Sebo* consists of some plain houses and only a few streets laid out at right angles, none of them paved.

But not everything has remained unscathed. There are a few restaurants, which cater for the needs of the many day-trippers. Practically every house has apartments to let, there is a

Fresh and dried fish for sale in Órzola

well-stocked supermarket and even a disco. But none of this compares with Lanzarote-style mass tourism. The *Playa de Francesa*, the *Playa de la Cocina* and, above all, the *Playa de las Conchas* (see p. 60) in the north rank among the finest and most isolated beaches in the Canaries. La Graciosa continues to be an island haven reserved for a few beach joggers, walkers, birdwatchers and lovers of peace and quiet – at least for the time being.

Passenger ferries (no vehicle transport): *Líneas Marítimas Romero (daily from Órzola at 8.30am, 10am, 11am, noon, 1.30pm, 4pm, 5pm and 6pm; from La Graciosa at 8am, 10am, 11am, 12.30pm, 3pm, 4pm and 5pm, additional connections in the summer | return crossing 20 euros, with bus transfer from the hotels in the resorts 29 euros | tel. 902 40 16 66 | lineasromero.com).*

EATING & DRINKING

If you're not a fish fan, you might be at a loss on the island. All restaurants serve fresh fish *a la plancha* (cooked on a hot metal skillet). *El Varadero (€€)* offers views of the harbour, while the *Girasol Playa (€€)* is perched right above the beach. It goes without saying that Romero, the owner of the mini-ferry fleet, is also a player on the gastronomic scene. Rather fittingly, his restaurant is called *El Marinero (€€)* – "The Sailor".

SPORT & ACTIVITIES

There is a wide selection of hikes to choose from on La Graciosa. Hikers who consider themselves to be in good shape could climb either of the following volcanoes from its less steep side: the *Montaña del Mojón* in the middle of the island and the *Montaña Bermeja* in the north. The two varied circular walks described below may be undertaken independently. Neither is too strenuous.

NORTHERN ROUTE

A track leads through the middle of the island from Caleta del Sebo and between the two volcanic cones of the Montaña del Mojón and the Agujas Grandes and then straight through to the  *Playa de las Conchas*. This beach must be one of the finest on the Canary Islands with Caribbean white sand and flanked by cliffs. The view of the offshore island of Montaña Clara is absolutely stunning. But because of the strong waves and currents the waters here are dangerous even for experienced swimmers. Plus, there are no lifeguards here. Below the Montaña Bermeja turn towards the north coast to reach the spectacular dunes near *Playa Lambra*. You can't miss the astonishing sight of countless millions of snail shells, in places completely covering the surface of the sand. Return to the harbour at Caleta via the village of *Pedro Barba*, which is not permanently inhabited. *Approx. 16km or 4 hrs*

SOUTHERN ROUTE

If you choose the southern route, leave Caleta del Sebo along the harbour basin. When you reach the pretty *Playa del Salado*, look out for a track, which you should follow. If walking in the hot sun, it's worth going a little further south for two even more beautiful beaches, the *Playa Francesa*

and the *Playa de la Cocina*. Both are covered in beautifully soft, white sand leading out into crystal-clear water. Now return a short distance and on the shore side pass below the *Montaña Amarilla*, the "Yellow Mountain", to reach the west coast. There you will join a track, which first passes vegetable fields and then, keeping the Montaña del Mojón always on the right-hand side, returns to Caleta del Sebo. *Approx. 10km or 2.5 hrs*

TEGUISE

(⬚ *F7–8*) **When you arrive in ★ ⚑ Teguise (pop. 17,000), it will seem as if you have made a journey back in time. You will be greeted by grand villas with high**

wooden portals and then have to squeeze through narrow alleyways to reach imposing churches and broad plazas.

There is very little evidence that almost 600 years have passed since the founding of the Real Villa, the royal town of Teguise. Maciot de Béthencourt built the first colonial town on the Canary Islands in 1428, on the site of an even older Majo settlement, and named it after his wife, a Majo princess. Teguise remained the capital of the island until 1852. Powerful families, such as the Herreras and Feo Perazas, built their townhouses here.

But why up there so far from the coast? This is a good question, as cool trade winds blow through the streets, clouds often shroud the town in mist and it is always cooler than by the sea. But the early inhabitants had good

reason to choose this settlement. During the winter the vital rain falling on the neighbouring mountain of Guanapay was collected in a giant underground cistern, the *Gran Mareta*. Furthermore, the Spanish colonials felt safer away from the coast given the threat of pirate attacks. The protection offered by the powerful castle, the Castillo Santa Bárbara built nearby on Guanapay, gave added protection.

But they were mistaken. Teguise was repeatedly attacked from the sea. A plaque in the *Callejón de Sangre* ("Blood Alley") behind the Church of Nuestra Señora de Guadalupe recalls a massacre carried out by the feared Algerian buccaneers in 1586. In 1618, pirates burned the place to the ground; the oldest surviving buildings date from the 17th century. But that doesn't take anything away from their splendour. The historic centre of

Explore La Graciosa on foot to see the best of the island

the town with its unique architectural style has been under a preservation order since 1973.

Now Teguise leads a double life. The atmosphere on weekdays is relaxed. Locals as well as the many foreigners who live here sit next to the odd day tripper or two at one of the stylish or trendy cafés before they browse through the nice shops. But on Sunday it's market day and the place comes alive and almost bursts at the seams. The *mercadillo* here is one of Lanzarote's main attractions. Holidaymakers arrive in their thousands; countless traders, here to peddle kitsch and knick-knacks from all over the world, also descend on the town. Folk groups are on hand to entertain the throngs of visitors. The streets and the squares, the whole town in fact, resembles an oriental bazaar. In the bars, shoppers jostle for drinks, which are often much dearer on that day than elsewhere on the island. The Gran Mareta, the rather forlorn plaza above the ancient cisterns behind the church, is jam-packed with takeaway food stalls. Although all the bustle has very little to do with day-to-day life on the island, the *mercadillo* is something to behold, as there is nothing quite so hectic and chaotic anywhere else on Lanzarote. And then by Sunday evening Teguise has returned to its slumbers to resume its leisurely pace come Monday.

SIGHTSEEING

CASTILLO SANTA BÁRBARA
Even from a distance, the fortress brings to mind knights and buccaneers. It can be reached via a tarmac road, which branches off to the right from the road to Haría at the town edge. This fortress was built in the 16th century to protect the islanders from pirate attacks. Sometimes up to 1,000 people sought refuge within its walls. The entrance is a separate stone staircase with drawbridge. The fortress now houses the 👁 *Museo de la Piratería (daily 10am–4pm | admission 3 euros, children free | museodela pirateria.com | ⟳ 30 mins).* Model ships, cannons and weapons remind visitors of the raids Lanzarote endured. Take the opportunity to go up onto the roof for a magnificent view over the northern half of the island.

LA CILLA
This former tithe house, built in the 17th century, was the collecting point for the corn tax, which Lanzarote had to pay to the bishop on Gran Canaria. Now it houses a large arts and crafts shop.

CONVENTO DE SAN FRANCISCO
A museum of sacred art has taken up residence in the former convent church. Dramatically staged, expressive sculptures of saints are everywhere. The architecture is also worth a closer look: the ornate wooden ceilings soaring above the naves are simply breathtaking! *Tue–Sat 9.30am–4.30pm, Sun 10am–2pm | admission 2 euros | Plaza San Francisco | ⟳ 20 mins.*

Locals and tourists flock to Teguise for the Sunday market

CONVENTO DE SANTO DOMINGO

Art in a church can also be viewed in this former Dominican monastery. Magnificent wooden ceilings, white-washed walls and a showy, colourful rococo altar form the backdrop for changing exhibitions. *Sun–Fri 10am–3pm | admission 1.50 euros | ⏱ 15 mins.*

GRAN MARETA

This cistern, once the largest on Lanzarote, was built to store rainwater. Later it silted up. When the desalination plants were commissioned, it was surplus to requirements and was concreted over. Now the broad plaza behind the church is used to stage outdoor events and as space for the Sunday market.

IGLESIA DE NUESTRA SEÑORA DE GUADALUPE

This is the place to find some peace and quiet if you have come to the busy Sunday market. This parish church on the Plaza de la Constitución was consecrated in the 15th century, destroyed by pirates in 1680, then subsequently rebuilt. It is dedicated to Our Lady of Guadalupe, who is revered in Spain and in South America. Inside the bright naves, the colourfully painted figures of saints will catch your eye. The impressive façade with its huge stone tower contributes to the beautiful atmosphere on the plaza.

PALACIO MARQUÉS DE HERRERA Y ROJAS

This rather nondescript palace (1455) has a fine, covered inner courtyard. An exhibition of pieces made by the local craft school occupies the vestibule. Admission is free, but not all rooms are open to the public. *Mon–Fri 8am–3pm | C/ José Betancort*

A lion guards the parish church on Teguise's Plaza de la Constitución

PALACIO DE SPÍNOLA/CASA-MUSEO DEL TIMPLE

A house for nobility with a surprising interior. This old palace on the plaza, built between 1730 and 1780, is the prized gem in old Teguise. Particularly impressive are the interior courtyards, the chapel and the original kitchen. But even more noteworthy is the timple museum housed in the stately rooms of the Palacio de Spínola. Stringed instruments from around the world related to the Canarian timple (a five-stringed instrument resembling a ukulele) are on display and their sounds fill the rooms.

A workshop is set up to show just how much work goes into making these instruments. Once in a while, masters of the timple play concerts for the public. *Mon–Sat 9am–4.30pm, Sun 9am–3.30pm | admission 3 euros, children under 12 free | casadel timple.org | ⏱ 30 mins.*

PLAZA DE LA CONSTITUCIÓN

Around the central square in Teguise are some of the finest examples of colonial architecture: the Iglesia de Nuestra Señora de Guadalupe, the former La Cilla granary and tithe house and the Palacio de Spínola guarded by two lions. The palm and laurel trees provide some shade.

EATING & DRINKING

ACATIFE

A classic among Lanzarote's restaurants in a venerable building. Traditional, hearty fare. Try the rabbit in red wine sauce *(conejo al vino tinto). Closed Mon | C/ San Miguel 4 | tel. 928 84 50 37 | €€*

BODEGA SANTA BÁRBARA

Wine and snacks served in the little patio of this small bodega; inside there are more dishes and a mouth-watering range of tapas in the display cabinet. *Closed Tue | C/ La Cruz 5 | tel. 928 59 48 41 | €€*

LA CANTINA

Rich in tradition, this "canteen" in a historic house dishes up Canarian home-style cooking with a twist. It often plays host to live bands at the weekend. *Daily 11am–11pm | C/ León y Castillo 8 | mobile tel. 620 85 60 64 | cantinateguise.com | €–€€*

HESPÉRIDES

Located in an old townhouse (Casa León), this small restaurant serves imaginative dishes conjured from local produce. Ask the chef for his recommendation of the day, but you can't go wrong with olive bread and tapas, goat cheese and ham – all beautifully presented. *Closed Sun evening | C/ León y Castillo 3 | tel. 928 59 31 59 | hesperides-restaurant.negocio.site | €€*

IKARUS

Dine on unusual tapas and enjoy good island wine at this gastro bar on the atmospheric square. A salsa band plays in the courtyard during the Sunday market. *Closed Mon | Plaza Clavijo y Fajardo 6 | tel. 928 84 57 01 | €€*

SHOPPING

Teguise has always been an important centre of Canarian culture. And in recent years more and more artists and artisans from central Europe have moved to the island. The town's shops stock a large selection of crafts, jewellery and paintings.

LA LONJA EXCLUSIVA

This small shop sells approved copies of works by César Manrique. *Plaza de 18 de Julio*

MERCADILLO

The large Sunday market is the perfect place for browsers. Here you can find everything from art and arty knick-knacks to everyday items such as second-hand clothing, shoes and fresh fruit. Delicious farm produce is also on sale: *chorizo*, the piquant pork sausage with dried red peppers, or *turrón*, a nougat dessert with almonds. Exotic schnapps, liqueurs and jams are also on offer – and almost always with free samples! Buses leave from the holiday centres and Arrecife, and there's parking (charges payable) on the edge of the town. *Sun 9am–2pm*

TIMPLE WORKSHOP ANTONIO LEMES HERNÁNDEZ ⚑

Antonio Lemes Hernández is one of the last craftsmen making the famous Canarian guitar, the timple. For almost all his life he has been in his workshop piecing together every month the parts for about 15 different instruments of varying sizes, from the mini-timple to the contra-timple. They make a beautiful but expensive souvenir. The standard instrument costs around 200 euros; more elaborate models with pearl inlays and marquetry 400–500 euros. *C/ Flores 8*

AROUND TEGUISE

7 LAGOMAR ♀

2km south of Teguise / 5 mins by car via the LZ 10

Hidden away in a former quarry in Nazaret is this eccentric, fortress-like estate. Its first owner, in the 1970s, was the actor Omar Sharif (of *Dr Zhivago* fame) who is said to have gambled it away in a game of bridge.

Now the place is home to, among other things, a *museum (Tue–Sun 10am–6pm | admission 6 euros | ⊙ 30 mins)*. You can walk through caves and tunnels, set at different levels around an artificial pond, as you pass the Sharif Room. On display here are posters recalling the great actor's heyday; there is even a photo of that fateful card game. During the day, the *café-restaurant (closed Mon | €–€€)* serves tapas and daily specials, but in the evening upmarket Mediterranean cuisine takes over. An upscale lounge ambiance prevails in the cave bar *La Cueva (closed Mon)*. After 8pm, refined lighting and sound effects make for a magical evening. ▯ *F8*

8 LA CALETA DE FAMARA

12km north of Teguise / 15 mins by car via the LZ 402

A popular spot for surfers and a hideaway for those wishing to shun mass tourism is *La Caleta de Famara*. There are several bars and restaurants here. Surfers often take breakfast in the 🐟 *Croissantería (daily | €)*. For the best view, try the *Restaurante El Risco (closed Mon | C/ Montaña Clara 36 | tel. 928 52 85 50 | restauranteelrisco.com | €€€)*, which once belonged to a brother of César Manrique. It is now in the hands of a different proprietor and has been smartened up. What remains is the blue and white paint, the magnificent panorama of the Famara cliffs and the ever-present sound of the crashing ocean waves.

Try *El Sibarita (closed Mon | Av. El Marinero 128, to the west of the town | tel. 928 52 85 31 | €–€€)* for a healthy and reasonably priced meal. Lipez and Eduardo serve veggie and vegan dishes in this trendy eatery, including quinoa schnitzel and tofu burgers, great salads and *gofio* crêpes with cactus jam – plus, everything's available to take away. Wines, including organic wines, from the island as well as a wide range of herbal teas to aid digestion are also on offer.

INSIDER TIP
Veggies welcome!

🐟 *Playa de Famara* claims the title of Lanzarote's longest beach. It is also beautifully set, with the rugged Famara mountains below and surrounded as it is by dunes and the wild Atlantic. That said, it's too dangerous for swimming. The red flag is almost always up, signalling "No swimming"! Dangerous currents claim lives every year. ▯ *F–G6*

9 ERMITA DE LAS NIEVES

13km north of Teguise / 10 mins by car via the LZ 10 mountain road

This whitewashed pilgrimage chapel stands high up on the Risco de Famara.

The chapel is dedicated to the Virgen de las Nievas or Our Lady of the Snows, who has over the years received countless pleas for rain to fall on Lanzarote. Although the chapel is usually closed (Mass Sat 5pm), the long climb is still worth the effort, if only to see one of the finest panoramic views on the island. The cliffs drop almost vertically 600m into the sea. The islands of La Graciosa and Montaña Clara, the Playa de Famara, Teguise and the Timanfaya volcanoes are all clearly visible. *G7*

⑩ HARÍA ★

18km north of Teguise / 18 mins by car via the LZ 10 mountain road

When suddenly you descend into the valley of a thousand palms at the foot of the Famara mountain range, the scene is more Africa than Europe. Countless broad-crowned Canarian palms stand proudly among the low, white houses. Haría (pop. 5,000) is the friendliest place on Lanzarote. It is where you will see how *Lanzaroteños* used to live. So, it's no surprise that César Manrique retired to Haría and is buried here. His house, a traditional Lanzarote-style residence, is open to the public. It seems as if the man himself has just left the luxurious living quarters and the atelier in the *Casa Museo César Manrique (daily 10.30am–6pm | C/ Elvira Sánchez 30 | admission 10 euros | fcmanrique.org)*.

Take a stroll through the village to discover old villas with luxuriant green patios, small shops and bars in dreamy side streets. The *Plaza León y Castillo* with its shady weeping fig trees opens out in front of the church and is the perfect place for a break. The small *Museo Sacro Popular* on the

Snow white: there are stunning sea views from the Ermita de las Nieves

Look out over La Graciosa from Mirador del Río

square near the church displays sacred sculptures and paintings in a beautiful old house, but it is only open during the Saturday market.

People gather in the *Taller Municipal de Artesanía* craft centre *(summer Mon–Sat 10am–1pm and 3–5pm, winter 10am–1pm and 4–6pm)* near the Plaza de la Constitución to work on embroidery and shawls in keeping with the old tradition. These labour-intensive goods are sold at the *Saturday market (mercadillo)* and you will see many more artisans selling their wares here too. Also on sale here are home-made speciality food and drinks, such as organic goat's cheese from Haría. Temporary exhibitions are held in the 🐦 *El Aljibe gallery (admission*

INSIDER TIP
Goats and more goats!

free / open sporadically), formerly the water reservoir beneath the Plaza de la Constitución.

A good place for a coffee is 🐦 *La Sociedad Bar Tegala (daily | tel. 696 90 06 52 | €)* on the shady plaza. For finer dining, the best place to eat is *Puerta Verde (daily 1–10pm | C/ Fajardo 24 | tel. 928 83 53 50 | €€)*: The pasta, ice cream and cakes are all home-made and the dishes are seasoned with fresh herbs from the garden. *🚎 G6*

INSIDER TIP
Wild aroma

⓫ MIRADOR DE GUINATE 🐦
23.5km north of Teguise / 20 mins by car via the LZ 10/ LZ 201 mountain road
The view from the Mirador de Guinate near the village of the same name is no less spectacular than the view from

the Mirador del Río (see right) – but free. *G5*

12 MIRADOR DEL RÍO ★

27.5km north of Teguise / 25 mins by car via the LZ 10 / LZ 201 mountain road

Stunning is the only word to describe the view from this former fortification, the Batería del Río, perched precariously on a cliff top at a height of 479m in the far north of Lanzarote. The view extends as far as the islands of La Graciosa and Alegranza. Why not enjoy a drink and let it all sink in a little longer! Dating from 1974, the mirador complex was one of César Manrique's first works. It fits perfectly into the environment. *Daily 10am–5.45pm | admission 4.75 euros | ⊙ 30 mins | G4–5*

13 YÉ

26km north of Teguise / 25 mins by car via the LZ 10/ LZ 201 mountain road

The village of Yé clings to the mountainside at a height of around 400m beneath the impressive panorama of the eroded Monte Corona. The *Volcán de la Corona* restaurant *(closed Mon | tel. 928 52 65 16 | €€)* near the junction to the Mirador del Río is recommended. Continuing towards Órzola/Arrieta, you will see the road to the quaint winery *Bodega Monte Corona (daily 11am–6pm).* Here you can taste local wines as well as cactus liqueur – it's wonderfully purple and is slightly tart. From harvesting to first pressing and bottling, everything is still done by hand and no synthetic additives are used here. *G5*

INSIDER TIP
Quaff some colour

WHERE TO SLEEP IN THE NORTH

A LOTUS LULLABY

If you're in search of a quiet night, you won't find better on Lanzarote than *Lotus del Mar (C/ El Cangrejo 31 | tel. 928 52 95 89 | lotusdelmar. com | €-€€),* with its comfortable Manrique-style apartments and *casitas.* The gleaming white exterior hides a lovingly furnished, well-designed and airy interior. Choose Marlene or Santa María to be in one of the houses closest to the sea.

PUERTO DEL CARMEN & THE CENTRE

VINEYARDS, FARMING & TOURISM

On this skilfully worked farmland, grapes are grown commercially. Thousands of vines, each with its own small crater, thrive despite the harsh conditions.

The bright green vine grows in a pit about 2m deep, surrounded by a layered, semi-circular wall of grey stone. The green leaves stand out so starkly against the black soil that the vine could almost be a cheap plastic imitation.

Science fiction? No, these are vineyards in a lava field

The vine-growing region extends across this lowland strip like the work of a graphic designer. As far as the coast between La Santa and Sóo, old traditions linger among the people and on the land. The deliciously fruity tomatoes and the searingly hot onions, which add character to the local *ensalada mixta*, come from these parts.

Meanwhile, a completely different world has emerged on the east coast in Puerto del Carmen – a shrine to tourism where absolutely everything is international, from the people to the food scene.

PUERTO DEL CARMEN & THE CENTRE

MARCO POLO HIGHLIGHTS

★ **LA GERIA**
In what is probably the world's most unusual wine-growing region, plenty of bodegas invite you to taste the local wines ➤ p. 79

★ **CASA MUSEO DEL CAMPESINO**
Artisans are busy in the workshops at this "House of the Farmer", which is inspired by traditional architecture ➤ p. 80

★ **MUSEO AGRÍCOLA EL PATIO**
The island's farming history lives on here: dromedaries pull the plough and the bodega looks like it did 100 years ago ➤ p. 81

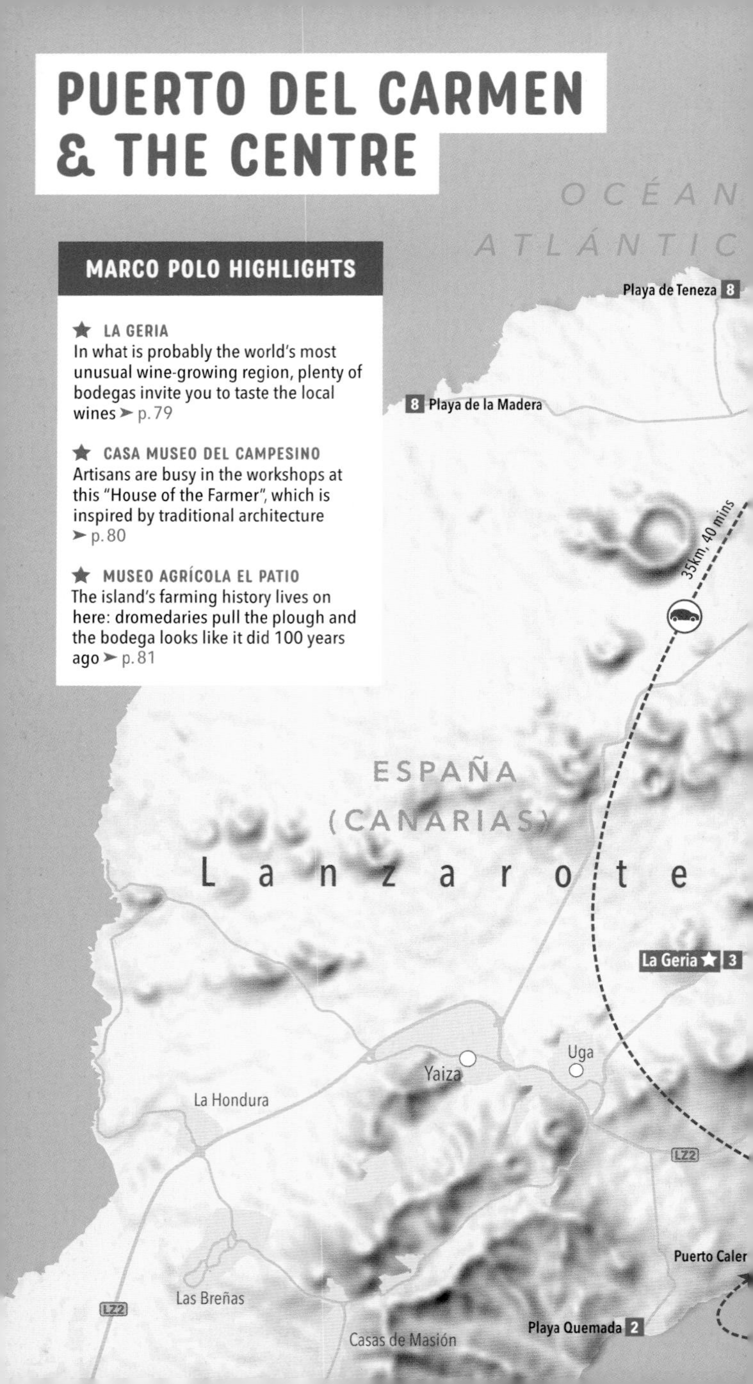

OCÉAN
ATLÁNTIC

Playa de Teneza 8

8 Playa de la Madera

35 km, 40 mins

ESPAÑA
(CANARIAS)

L a n z a r o t e

La Geria ★ 3

Uga

Yaiza

La Hondura

LZ2

Puerto Caler

LZ2

Las Breñas

Casas de Masión

Playa Quemada 2

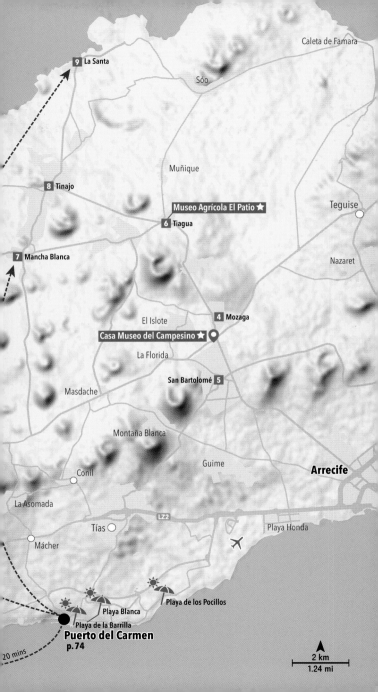

Caleta de Famara

9 La Santa

Sóo

Muñique

Teguise

8 Tinajo

Museo Agrícola El Patio ★

6 Tiagua

Nazaret

7 Mancha Blanca

El Islote

4 Mozaga

Casa Museo del Campesino ★

La Florida

San Bartolomé **5**

Masdache

Montaña Blanca

Guime

Arrecife

Conil

La Asomada

Tías

LZ2

Playa Honda

Mácher

Playa de los Pocillos

Playa Blanca

Playa de la Barrilla

Puerto del Carmen
p.74

20 mins

2 km
1.24 mi

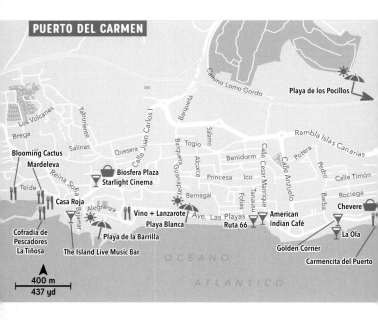

PUERTO DEL CARMEN

(🗺 D10) **The former fishing village of Puerto del Carmen (pop. 3,000) has blossomed into a top-class tourist centre. The village divides up into an older quarter around the fishing harbour and a vast expanse of holiday villages with 35,000 beds to the north.**

The main reason behind the rapid development of this small town into a major resort is the splendid beaches blessed with clean water. Above them, the traffic-reduced *Avenida de las Playas* stretches for 7km along the coast. The eye delights in the green of the palms and the yellow of the sand

near the coast, while inland it is met by an endless chain of bars and restaurants, arcades and smaller shopping centres. If one long party on the promenade is not for you, head for the upper town or seek out one of the big hotels facing away from the road. There you can enjoy your holiday undisturbed.

Puerto del Carmen has something for everyone. In the old town by the fishing harbour, the everyday life of the locals takes centre-stage. Just as they have done for centuries, the fishermen will be out in the morning by their boats sorting through last night's catch. Throughout the day there always seems to be a few anglers whiling away their time on the quayside and in the evening groups of men armed with metal balls assemble for a round of pétanque. And if Mass is about to start in the small chapel of Nuestra Señora del Carmen, which is tucked away among all the fish restaurants, the faithful will be hurrying along the street – locals and visitors alike.

EATING & DRINKING

Tourist hotspot Puerto del Carmen claims to have more than 200 restaurants. But not all of them are recommended. Many, particularly along Avenida de las Playas, are interested only in a rapid turnover. If you want original Canarian dishes, perhaps with locally caught fish, it's better to look around the fishing harbour.

BLOOMING CACTUS

Greek-inspired tapas hit the tables at this vegetarian/vegan bistro above the harbour – healthy, fresh and tasty! *Tue–Sun from 6pm | C/ Teide 35 | tel. 608 29 38 37 | bloomingcactus.co.uk | €*

CARMENCITA DEL PUERTO

Álvaro and Irena have nailed it: cheery atmosphere, freshly made imaginative tapas and friendly service. But best to book as there are only seven terrace tables! *Mon–Sat from 7pm | Av. de las Playas | CC Marítimo | tel. 928 51 23 18 | €€*

CASA ROJA

There's hardly a better way of watching the sun go down or place for a romantic meal. You sit on a long and narrow terrace a few metres above the water in the old harbour basin. *Daily | Av. del Varadero 22 | tel. 928 51 07 03 | €€*

COFRADÍA DE PESCADORES LA TIÑOSA

The fishermen always bring their catches to their cooperative (cofradía) first. The fish are cleaned and gutted right before the tables on the terrace and then fried a la plancha (on a hot metal skillet). You can't get any closer to the boats as they come and go. *Daily | Plaza del Varadero | tel. 660 43 35 78 | €€*

MARDELEVA

Although quiet, this restaurant still has a view of the sea thanks to its hidden location above the harbour. Enjoy tasty fish dishes, solid tapas and Lanzarote wines as the fresh Atlantic

Fishing boats can still be seen in the harbour at Puerto del Carmen

Sunbathe and swim next to palm trees and lava cliffs

breeze brushes your skin. *Daily from 10.30am | C/ los Infantes 10 | tel. 928 51 06 86 | €€*

VINO + LANZAROTE

First, there was only a wine and gourmet foods shop, but then the visitors kept wanting to sample all the delicacies. And so Ms Hanneke and Señor Miguel opened a tapas bar next door where they offer the island's best wines, served by the glass, together with delicious tapas – from deep-fried aubergine with palm honey to Iberian ham. Live music is featured twice a week – be sure to make a reservation! *Closed Sun | C/ Timanfaya s/n, CC Playa Blanca L. 14 | tel. 928 51 69 59 | €*

INSIDER TIP
Wine & vibes

SHOPPING

BIOSFERA PLAZA

For shopaholics: you will find many Spanish-made products at the small but chic shopping centre made of chrome and glass: fashions from Blanco, Bershka, Sfera and Zara, leather accessories from Piel de Toro and cosmetics from Aloe Plus. *Av. Juan Carlos 15 | above the harbour | biosfera plaza.es*

CHEVERE

One of the few jewellery and souvenir stores to have escaped being "swallowed" by the Biosfera shopping centre! Also a good spot to find jewellery with the iridescent green stone olivine. *Av. de las Playas 45 | tel. 928 51 23 38 | FB: Chevere JR*

SPORT & ACTIVITIES

Is there anything more enjoyable to do on an island than take a boat trip? The water bus sails several times a day to the neighbouring coastal town of Puerto Calero *(6 euros one way | lineasromero.com)*. From there you can even transfer to a submarine. The yacht *Maype* can be booked for one- to six-hour boat trips *(incl. snorkelling tours and lunch, from 30 euros | seafunlanzarote.com)*. Adrenaline junkies can take to the air. You are attached to both a parachute and a line on a speedboat *(Paracraft Lanzarote | 50 euros/10 mins | Paseo de la Barilla | tel. 928 51 26 61 | water sports-lanzarote.com)*. The *Flyboard* costs twice as much and you have to be in pretty good shape. A lot cheaper are the 🐵 jet boat, banana boat and crazy UFO (which is great fun for kids!)

RANCHO TEXAS LANZAROTE PARK 🐵

An adventure and animal park for the whole family: parrots, birds of prey and sea lions perform at shows. Children love to play in the Sioux village and can search for gold treasure and go canoeing. The park is easily accessible by bus from hotels in Puerto del Carmen, Costa Teguise and Playa Blanca (see website). *Daily 9.30am–5.30pm | admission 30 euros, children (2–14 years) 22 euros | leave Puerto del Carmen on C/ Noruega and cross under the bypass | www. ranchotexaslanzarote.com | ⊙ half day | ▭ D 10*

BEACHES

Of the local beaches, the very best is 🌴 *Playa Blanca* (aka *Playa Grande*), more than 1km long, situated at the foot of low cliffs and dotted with shady palms. This beach is followed to the east by the even longer and less busy 🌴 *Playa de los Pocillos* and *Playa Matagorda*. You can rent loungers and umbrellas on all three beaches, and after 5pm you'll have the beaches pretty much to yourself. Even better, the sun loungers are free then!

INSIDER TIP
Sun loungers at sunset

As long as the normal trade winds are blowing, the currents at these beaches are mostly gentle and the wind and waves not very strong. This means that, in general, the waters are not dangerous for swimming – even for children. Small but nice is the partially hidden 🌴 *Playa de la Barrilla* near the harbour below the former town centre. Two rocky ridges flank this beach of fine sand.

NIGHTLIFE

Start off your evening at the old harbour and then head out to the Avenida de las Playas. This is the place to find the island's most varied nightlife.

AMERICAN INDIAN CAFÉ

Disco and cocktail bar for 30- to 50-year-olds with live shows and video clips on screens. *Daily 10am–3am | Av. de las Playas 35 | american-indian-cafe.com*

GOLDEN CORNER

A quiet place to relax and popular among people aged 30 or over for its large selection of cocktails. *Daily from 10pm | Av. de la Playas 16*

THE ISLAND LIVE MUSIC BAR

This is the place to be! International singers and songwriters give concerts above the old harbour and the audience moves to the music! *Fri– Wed from 8pm | C/ Tenerife | islandbar lanzarote.com*

LA OLA

Although "the wave" is open during the day, it is at its best in the evening when the red lighting accentuates the Moroccan-inspired interior. Relax on a Bali lounger above the sea or smoke a water pipe in the pavilion! *Daily from 10am | Av. de las Playas 10*

RUTA 66

This large disco/pub is the hottest spot in Puerto del Carmen. Opens out on to the promenade. Several bars, football on wide screens and dancing to US rock. *Daily from 10pm | CC Arena Dorada | Av. de las Playas*

STARLIGHT CINEMA

Watch a movie under the stars: English-language films are shown almost every evening on the rooftop terrace of the Biosfera Plaza shopping centre. Just lie back and order some drinks and snacks. *Daily 6.30pm and 8.45pm | CC Biosfera Plaza (5th level) | Av. Juan Carlos 15 | rooftopbiosfera. com*

AROUND PUERTO DEL CARMEN

1 PUERTO CALERO

3km west of Puerto del Carmen / 5 mins by car or 20 mins by waterbus

Many sailors stop off here on their way from Europe to America, but it's worth a visit even if you're not an ocean-going mariner. It is fun to stroll along the very elegant seafront promenade with its golden bollards and row of blue and white houses. Sailing trips, including five-hour catamaran tours, depart from here *(daily 11am–3.30pm | 39–64 euros | tel. 928 51 30 22 | cat-lanza.com)*. Another option is a descent to the seabed in a submarine: *Submarine Safaris (dives 10am, 11am, noon, 2pm | 55 euros, online reductions | tel. 928 51 28 89 | submarinesafaris.com)*. *Restaurant Amura (daily | tel. 928 51 31 81 | restauranteamura.com | €€€)* is a sophisticated option in the style of a southern villa with a large veranda and palm terrace at the end of the marina, offering imaginative fusion cuisine. The four-star hotel *Costa Calero (tel. 928 84 95 95 | hotelcosta calero.com)* also scores points with a spa that's also open to day guests. Inside, there's a frigidarium (18°C) and a caldarium (over 34°C) as well as a pool that flows through the garden, while hydro jets guarantee massages and fast currents. | *D10*

Bodegas around La Geria offer wine-tasting

❷ PLAYA QUEMADA

13km west of Puerto del Carmen / 15 mins by car via the LZ 2/LZ 706
.Quemada ("burnt") refers to the fact that the beach here is black and stony. There are a few houses and one or two Canarian restaurants but, apart from that, there's little to detain you. For this very reason it appeals to holiday-makers seeking peace and quiet. Beyond the rocky crest, which is flooded at high tide, there is another beach that's never crowded. If you would like to linger and explore the craggy coastline, try the offerings at *Restaurante Salmarina (Av. Marítima 13 | tel. 928 17 35 62 | salmarina restaurante.com | €€).* Sit here right by the water in a part-maritime, part-rustic ambience and enjoy good-quality fish and seafood without any frills.

How does thinly sliced octopus sound *(pulpo a la gallega)?* | 🗺 C11

❸ LA GERIA ★

8–15km north of Puerto del Carmen / 10–20 mins by car via the LZ 2 or LZ 30
The countryside around La Geria could be mistaken for the work of a brilliant landscape architect. The main route through the region runs from Mozaga in the centre of the island via Masdache as far as Uga in the south. The awesome vine region near the volcanic mountains appears to be even more intensively farmed when approached from the minor roads, such as from the road to La Vegueta. What is hard to believe is that nature itself initially brought new life to the barren land in the form of the delicate, grey-green lichen. Only much, much later did

farmers move into vegetable and fruit growing, creating new plots of arable land. The small lava grains that make up the soil play a vital role in the harvest in such a dry climate with strong trade winds. Incredibly porous, these little stones called lapilli suck moisture from the sea breeze that blows over La Geria at night and gradually release the water into the vine roots during the day. This unique method is the only way to cultivate fruit here.

The main bodegas are beside the main road, most of them opening from 10.30am to 6pm. The *El Grifo* winery *(LZ 30, Km11 | elgrifo.com)* has a wine museum *(admission 4 euros)* where tools, some of which are over 200 years old, are exhibited. The *Bodegas Barreto (LZ 30, Km11 | tel. 928 52 07 17)* offer a wide selection of wines from about 2 euros per glass (tasting included). The *Bodega La Geria (LZ 30, Km19 | lageria.com)* is situated directly opposite a fine dragon tree. If you take a tour through the *Bodegas Rubicón (LZ 30, Km19 | bodegasrubicon.com)*, a restored historic house, you will be shown the beautiful wine cellar and old presses before you can sample the wines. A somewhat primitive bodega a little out of the way but accessible via a rough track, ▰ *El Chupadero (Wed–Sun from noon | LZ 30, Km18.8 | tel. 928 17 31 15 | el-chupadero.com | €€)* has a cosy tapas bar with a terrace where you can unhurriedly snack on Mediterranean delicacies and sip the house wines. There is a view over thousands of mini-craters cradling the precious vines. ⬚ *C–E 9–10*

▰ MOZAGA

15km north of Puerto del Carmen / 15 mins by car via the LZ 2/LZ 35)

On the roundabout outside this village stands one of Manrique's largest pieces, the *Monumento al Campesino*, the "Monument to the Peasant Farmer". It was built at the end of the 1960s to draw attention to the worsening plight of the farmers. Appropriately it comprises water tanks from old fishing boats stacked together into a large, Cubist-inspired dromedary. It serves as a reminder that the island does not have an inexhaustible supply of resources.

Nearby is the ★ ▰ *Casa Museo del Campesino (daily 10am–5.45pm | admission free)*, a farmers' and arts and crafts museum where you can watch craftsmen and women at work and purchase their products. As well as watching embroiderers and weavers (only occasionally) at work, the activities in the pottery workshop are of special interest. The artisans here make *novios de mojón*: originally, these clay figure couples with their exaggerated sexual organs were made by the early inhabitants as fertility symbols and given to young newlyweds.

The lower part of the old farmhouse houses a restaurant *(daily | tel. 928 52 01 36 | €€)* in lava vaults, serving typical Lanzarotean dishes. In the cosier bar on the ground floor you can sit on a gleaming white terrace, view the *monument*, eat Lanzarotean tapas and enjoy a drink or two. ⬚ *E8*

Monumento al Campesino by César Manrique

5 SAN BARTOLOMÉ
12km northeast of Puerto del Carmen / 10 mins by car via the LZ 2/ LZ 35

A plaza with a church, the town hall and a theatre make this quiet municipality a pleasant place. Diagonally opposite the square, the house with striking murals is the private *Museo Etnográfico Tanit (Mon–Sat 10am–2pm | admission 6 euros | C/ Constitución 1 | museotanit.com)* with its lovingly created displays of artefacts, including tools, furniture, toys, clothes and carnival costumes from days gone by. Book-lovers trek to the town of Tías, 7km to the southwest, where the finca of the Nobel prize-winning author José Saramago (2022–2010) has been turned into a museum-like "house of books" called *A Casa José Saramago (Mon–Sat 10am–2.30pm,* *tours every 30 mins | admission 8 euros | C/ Los Topes 2 | Tías | tel. 928 83 35 26 | acasajosesaramago.com).* 🕮 *E9*

6 TIAGUA
20km northeast of Puerto del Carmen / 20 mins by car via the LZ 502/LZ 30/LZ 20)

You would probably drive right by the farming village if it weren't for the ★ *Museo Agrícola El Patio (Mon–Fri 10am–5pm, Sat 10am–2.30pm | admission 5 euros including a small sample of wine).* The museum is housed in an old, but well-preserved farmhouse and provides a glimpse into the traditions of the peasant farmers. All the displays, from the bodega to the *gofio* mill, are in full working order. Chickens are roaming about in the garden, goats bleat from the stables, and in the shade, a dromedary

INSIDER TIP
Museum with homemade goodies

and a donkey wait to be petted. Visit the windmill and the bodega, where you can sample wine and cheese. Old photographs and pottery that was used on the farm are displayed in the farmhouse. Also exhibited in the museum is a collection of beautiful lava stones and rocks. Adjoining the farmhouse are the old winery buildings with a collection of heavy presses and oak barrels. *E8*

7 MANCHA BLANCA

25km north of Puerto del Carmen / 30 mins by car via the LZ 504/LZ 502/ LZ 56)

In 1735 streams of lava poured out of the Timanfaya volcanoes and advanced relentlessly on the little village. In desperation the inhabitants made one final attempt to avert the imminent catastrophe: they placed a statue of the village patron saint, Nuestra Señora de los Dolores, in front of the glowing lava as it edged ever closer. And it worked. The molten lava came to a standstill right in front of the figure. By way of thanks, the villagers built the Iglesia de los Dolores on the edge of the village and proclaimed the Madonna to be Señora de los Volcanes – Our Lady of the Volcanoes. She then became the island's patron saint. On the road to Timanfaya National Park, you will pass the *Visitor Centre* (see p. 100). *D8*

8 TINAJO, PLAYA DE TENEZA & PLAYA DE LA MADERA

17–25km north of Puerto del Carmen /20–30 mins by car via the LZ 502/LZ 56/LZ 67)

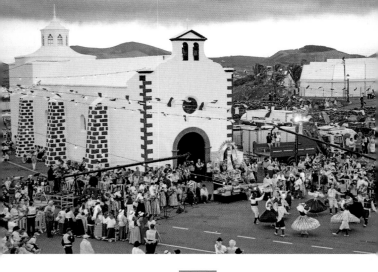

In September, Mancha Blanca celebrates its patron saint, La Virgen de los Dolores

Not spectacular, but rather pretty is the long and narrow village of *Tinajo* (□ D7). A good place to eat here is 🍴 *Mezzaluna (closed Mon | Av. La Cañada 22 | tel. 928 84 01 41 | €–€€)*, where all the Italian classics are served – and that means pizzas from a charcoal oven.

Some way from the centre of the village an unmarked road leads to the west coast and *Playa de Teneza* (□ C–D7), then on rough tracks to *Playa de la Madera* (□ B8) on the edge of Timanfaya National Park. The Atlantic waves often break powerfully on both beaches, with the seething waters making an impressive natural spectacle. If you swim here, stay in shallow waters. All too often bathers drown on the west coast, because they underestimate the immense suction power in the retreating sea and are dragged underwater.

Now drive towards Caleta de Famara. En route it is worth making the climb to the old mill. Stop for a minute and admire the impressive view over the village and the Risco de Famara mountain range.

�","9 LA SANTA

35km north of Puerto del Carmen / 40 mins by car via the LZ 50/LZ 56/LZ 67)

Every serious athlete has heard of this little hamlet on the northern coast. It is home to the training oasis *La Santa (tel. Mon–Fri 9am–5pm | www. clublaasanta.com/en)*, a club that offers dozens of sporting activities and has its own athletics stadium, wind-surfing lagoon and road-cycling base to name a few. For regular day trippers,

however, the nondescript town has little to offer other than a multitude of restaurants along the through road. The *Alma Tapas (closed Mon | Av. Marinero 26 | €€)* serves excellent snacks and daily specials in a pretty courtyard. □ D7

WHERE TO STAY IN THE CENTRE OF LANZAROTE

ESCAPE THE MAINSTREAM

Do you feel like unwinding and being creative at a hotel with a personal touch? Far above the hustle and bustle of the tourist centre of Puerto del Carmen lies the *Centro de Terapia Antroposófica (C/ Salinas 12 | Puerto del Carmen | tel. 928 51 28 42 | en.turismo-antroposofico-lanzarote.com | €€)*, offering 52 simply beautiful apartments clustered around an exotic pool garden. You can relax in the 34°C "floating pool" and try your hand at workshops ranging from painting to sculpture. The buffet includes a wide selection of vegetarian options and there is an organic supermarket for self-caterers.

AT THE HEART OF THE LAVA FIELDS

At the small inland hotel *Caserío de Mozaga (8 rooms | C/ Malva 8 | Mozaga | tel. 928 52 00 60 | caserio demozaga.com | €€€)* you can live as Lanzarote's lords once did: on a finca in a lava field with fig trees, shady patios and antique furnishings.

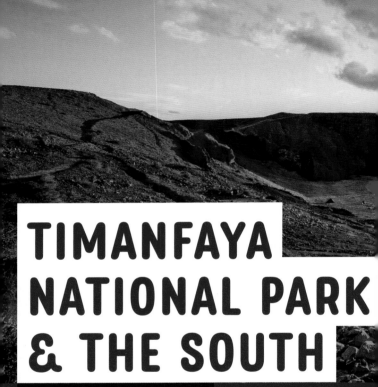

TIMANFAYA NATIONAL PARK & THE SOUTH

BEACHES & BLOWN TOPS

The south of Lanzarote is not unlike the Sahara Desert – barren land, parched by the sun, a few scrubby areas of lichen and dried grasses – and it can have a mesmerising effect. As the island's driest region, sunshine is guaranteed! And that is just one of the reasons why the fishing village of Playa Blanca has become one of the three big holiday hotspots.

This is where the Fire Mountains border the south with their seas of black lava and dozens of volcanoes, some with blown tops,

How romantic! Sunset at the Playas de Papagayo

others softly rising in every colour from beige to grey and deep rusty red.

Volcanic eruptions raged from 1730 to 1736, burying almost a quarter of the island and creating the world's largest lava field. Around a hundred years later, the earth started playing tricks once again, spewing yet more lava. Now, almost 200 years after the last catastrophe, you can safely explore the *malpaís* ("badlands") and plunge into the darkness on the Ruta de los Volcanes.

TIMANFAYA NATIONAL PARK & THE SOUTH

MARCO POLO HIGHLIGHTS

★ **MUSEO ATLÁNTICO DE LANZAROTE**
An artificial underwater world –
mysterious and beautiful ➤ p. 89

★ **PLAYAS DE PAPAGAYO**
Golden yellow jewels: Lanzarote's finest
beaches ➤ p. 93

★ **FEMÉS**
The far-reaching view from the *balcón* is
spectacular ➤ p. 94

★ **SALINAS DE JANUBIO**
The Canary Islands' largest salt pans
glisten in a multi-coloured array ➤ p. 95

★ **LOS HERVIDEROS**
The waves pound their way through
rocky channels amid mountains of spray
➤ p. 95

★ **CHARCO DE LOS CLICOS**
An otherworldly bottle-green lagoon
➤ p. 95

★ **ECHADERO DE LOS CAMELLOS**
A ride through the volcanic ash fields in
Timanfaya National Park on the back of
a dromedary is an amazing experience
➤ p. 99

★ **RUTA DE LOS VOLCANES**
The highlight of any visit to Timanfaya is
a tour through the park's lunar
landscape ➤ p. 100

El Gol

Charco de los Clicos ★ 7

Los Hervideros ★ 6

Salinas de Janubio ★

LZ2

OCÉANO
ATLÁNTICO

Montaña Roja 1

Faro de Pechiguera 2

10 Fuerteventura

Playa Blanca
● p. 88
Playa Dorada
Playa Flamingo

3.5km, 30 mins

Centro de Visitantes e Interpretación **13**
de Mancha Blanca

Parque Nacional de Timanfaya
p. 98

Ruta de los Volcanes ★ **12**

Echadero de Los Camellos ★ **11**

2 km, 20 mins

L a n z a r o t e

La Asomada

8 Yaiza

9 Uga

Honduras

E S P A Ñ A
(C A N A R I A S)

LZ2

Las Breñas

Puerto Calera

4 Femés ★

Playa Quemada

Casas de Masión

Museo Atlántico de Lanzarote ★

3 Playas de Papagayo ★

2 km
1.24 mi

PLAYA BLANCA

(🕮 A–B 11–12) **Once there was just a remote fishing village in this barren region; now there's a sprawling conurbation of white-washed holiday villages.**

The architecture of the villas and hotels is worth a closer look, and luxuriant gardens awash with colourful bougainvillea do wonders for the overall impression of Playa Blanca (pop. 10,000). The extensive resort which is spread out over a flat plain is perfect for everyone from families to elderly people. Its main advantages are proximity to the fantastic Playas de Papagayo and the almost unbroken sunshine.

The spacious, pedestrianised promenade is the heart of Playa Blanca. Here you can take a relaxed stroll while looking out to sea towards the neighbouring islands. The town beach has a family atmosphere, and the restaurants and apartments are restricted to a height of two or three storeys.

Heading westwards, the promenade continues for miles to the lighthouse, *Faro de Pechiguera*. To the east, it extends from the ferry port as far as the vast *Marina Rubicón* and the *Castillo de las Coloradas*. Unfortunately, over time, monumental hotels have begun to encroach on the paradise beaches. Row after row of villa and

Head to Marina Rubicón for a stroll or a night out

apartment complexes have slowly crept inland onto the parched plain.

SIGHTSEEING

MARINA RUBICÓN & CASTILLO DE LAS COLORADAS
Follow the promenade eastwards and you will first pass *Playa Dorada*, then the *Marina Rubicón*. Here terraced cafés, water features and pontoons that jut out over the sea make for a relaxed and elegant atmosphere. Still further east along the promenade, the *Castillo de las Coloradas* comes into view. Yes, even down here on the south coast, the fishing communities were not immune from pirate attacks, and the villages were repeatedly pillaged. It is said that the conqueror Jean de Béthencourt once built a fortress here.

The present castle dates from 1769. Its name derives from the colourful *(coloradas)* rocks along the coast. Unfortunately, the massive circular tower is not open to visitors and is now partially blocked off by hotels. It is worth making the trip to the Punta del Águila promontory for fine views along the colourful cliffs as far as the nearby Papagayo beaches, over the Marina Rubicón and, if the weather is fine, to Fuerteventura.

MUSEO ATLÁNTICO DE LANZAROTE ★
Have you ever wanted to dive into a museum? Now you can at Europe's first undersea museum: 400 quite realistic, life-sized concrete figures are waiting for you at a depth of 12–15m.

British artist Jason deCaires Taylor arranged the figures in everyday situations: refugees on the "Raft of Lampedusa", a couple taking a selfie, people crowding in front of a wall... The artist hopes that an artificial reef full of diverse species of fish will someday evolve as aquatic plants take over the sculptures. On calm days when the water is clear, it is possible to look down at the exhibits from a boat. Otherwise, dive down or snorkel! A visit to the museum must be booked through an authorised diving school. But that is not a problem: practically all diving schools on Lanzarote offer the tour, e.g. *Windblue Sports* (see p. 91). *Daily from Marina Rubicón 10am–4pm | admission for divers 12 euros, for snorkelers 8 euros, plus the obligatory organised dive starting at 30 euros (approx. 2–3 hrs) | cact lanzarote.com/cact/museo-atlantico*

EATING & DRINKING

BAR ONE
Whatever the time of day, this is the perfect place to chill out over a snack, while watching the yachts come and go. ☛ Inexpensive lunchtime menu. *Daily | Marina Rubicón | tel. 928 34 99 30 | €–€€*

BODEGÓN LAS TAPAS
Tapas are consumed in large quantities in a rustic setting surrounded by wine barrels and overlooking the promenade and the sea. *Closed Sun | Paseo Marítimo 5 | tel. 928 51 83 10 | €–€€*

CASA BRÍGIDA 🚩
One of the island's well-known food experts, Pedro Santana, dons an apron himself in the kitchen of this restaurant serving creative and delicious Canarian cuisine. If you're not sure what to order, try the six-course set menu for 35 euros – you won't be disappointed! *Daily 1–11pm | Puerto Marina Rubicón, Local 32 B | tel. 928 51 91 90 | restaurantecasabrigida.com | €€*

LA CASA ROJA
The "Red House" with its panoramic windows sits on a wooden pier overlooking the marina crammed with smart yachts. The setting is elegant and the cuisine upmarket Mediterranean with an emphasis on fish and seafood. Recently, this classic go-to restaurant has met with increased criticism from diners. Nonetheless, it is still worth trying the parrotfish pâté and the squid carpaccio plus the *mojito* sorbet for dessert! *Daily | Marina Rubicón | tel. 928 51 96 44 | lacasaroja-lanzarote. com | €€*

LOS HERVIDEROS 🍽
It's not on the promenade and it can't boast sea views, but its low-budget lunchtime menus still draw crowds. *Closed Tue | C/ El Marisco 9 | tel. 928 51 77 07 | €*

SEBASTYAN'S
Done all in blue and white, this elegant restaurant is situated high above the promenade. From its lofty vantage point you can see all the way to Fuerteventura as you enjoy wonderfully prepared classics of Greek/Mediterranean cuisine. The restaurant also has a wine cellar with a large selection of wines. Be sure to make a reservation for the evening. *Daily | CC La Mulata L. 4 | C/ Lanzarote (direction of the lighthouse) | tel. 928 34 96 79 | sebastyans.com | €€*

> **INSIDER TIP**
> **The Med in the Atlantic**

SHOPPING

In search of a summer outfit or souvenir? Shops line the pedestrian-friendly street Calle Limones.

FUNDACIÓN CÉSAR MANRIQUE
More from the grand master, even here in Playa Blanca. *Av. Papagayo 8*

MERCADILLO
A small market surrounded by the lovely ambiance of the yacht harbour where you can buy local arts and crafts. In the marina, looking and browsing is half the fun! Find cosmetics made from aloe vera, textiles dyed with cochineal, island delicacies and so much more. *Wed and Sat 9am–2pm | Costa Papagayo and Marina Rubicón*

MODA INDIGO
Light fabrics are the stuff of modern fashion – at least on Lanzarote. Locally based designers, such as Romy B, design casual collections and accessories in high-quality linen. *C/ Limones 56 | romyb.info*

> **INSIDER TIP**
> **Ibiza-style made in Lanzarote**

Browse the market stalls on Playa Blanca's promenade

MYSTIC
Pamper yourself, but with natural materials: sponges, brushes and beach towels. *Av. Marítima*

SPORT & ACTIVITIES

AQUALAVA WATERPARK
Water slides, wet castles, a lazy river and artificial waves can be found just behind the beach of Playa Flamingo. *Daily | admission 21 euros, children 14.50 euros | C/ Gran Canaria 26 | in the Relaxia Lanzasur complex | aqualava.net*

BOAT TRIPS
On days when the ocean is calm, the harbour of Playa Blanca becomes the starting point for a number of different tours. A taxi boat leaves several times a day via Marina Rubicón (stop-over possible) to Playas de Papagayo and back *(15 euros, children 8 euros | excursionslanzarote.com)*. Boats from *Líneas Romero (express waterbus 15 euros, children 8 euros | lineasromero. com)* also sail the same route. The underwater world leisurely glides by beneath the glass-bottom boats of Líneas Romero as they head for the neighbouring island of *Fuerteventura (incl. time on shore and snorkelling break 44 euros, children 25 euros)*. The little ferry of the same operator sets course for Fuerteventura several times a day *(ticket 27 euros, children 15 euros)*. Or you can watch whales and dolphins from the deck of a sailing ship *(tour 75 euros, children 50 euros | cetaceosynavegacion.com)*.

WATER SPORTS
Kayak tours, SUP and snorkelling sessions are offered by Windblue Sports *(C/ Los Bebederos 20 | tel. 928*

Enjoy golden sand and calm seas at the Playas de Papagayo

51 96 06 | *windbluesports.com)*; they also run a scuba diving base *(windbluediving.com)*. You can hire a pedalo *(6 euros per person | on Playa Dorada)* or have fun on a jet ski or banana boat at Marina Rubicón *(banana boat 15 euros for 10 mins, jet ski for 20 mins, 2 people 6 euros | watersports-lanzarote.com)*.

BEACHES

There are three fine bathing beaches in the resort itself: the small, sandy beach beneath the promenade near the town centre; *Playa Flamingo* to the west, beneath Lanzarote Park hotel; and *Playa Dorada* east of the town beach. The two last-named beaches have fine, golden sand as well as loungers and parasols for hire. Breakwaters ensure safe bathing. The neigbouring *Playas de Papagayo* (see p. 93) are even nicer.

WELLNESS

All four- and five-star hotels in Playa Blanca have modern spa facilities. The town's no. 1 spa is at the *Hotel Princesa Yaiza (Av. Papagayo 22 | princesayaiza.com)*, where the health and beauty team use ingredients sourced on the island. The emphasis is on treatments that follow correct medical and cosmetic guidelines. All therapists are professionally trained and multilingual.

NIGHTLIFE

It's fun to sit and drink a glass of wine or a beer on the promenade and follow it with a cocktail in the marina. Just a few steps away, you can listen to live music ranging from flamenco to funk every evening after 8pm at the *Blue Note Club (bluenotelanzarote. com)*. From Thursday to Saturday evening, it's worth going to the stylish *Jazz Club Cuatro Lunas* in the Hotel Princesa Yaiza. Expect to hear top-class live music or themed parties from "Halloween" to "Fiesta Cubana".

On the other side of the town centre, towards the Faro de Pechiguera, *Marea Lounge Club (daily until 3.30am)* in the Centro Comercial La Mulata provides a green terrace on the promenade, the ideal place to chill out and watch the sun set over Fuerteventura. Live music afterwards.

IDER TIP
The perfect hangout

AROUND PLAYA BLANCA

1 MONTAÑA ROJA

2.8km northwest of Playa Blanca / 30 mins on foot

If visitors to Playa Blanca need some exercise, it's not far to Montaña Roja. It is a quick, easy climb (but without any shade) to the top of the Red Mountain (194m), the nearest volcano to Playa Blanca, and the only elevation on the southern El Rubicón plain. The ascent starts above the Montaña Baja holiday complex along a well-worn, easily visible footpath and it takes not much longer than half an hour.

At the top there is an equally good footpath around the entire crater. The view from up here encompasses Playa Blanca and the Papagayo beaches, to the south Fuerteventura is usually clearly visible. Further west, endless apartment blocks, some only half-finished, spoil the panoramic view. *A11*

2 FARO DE PECHIGUERA

3km west of Playa Blanca / 60 mins on foot

Playa Blanca's promenade leads westward to the Faro de Pechiguera along the coast and past Playa Flamingo. Built in 1986, the lighthouse is not in itself particularly impressive, but the view over to Fuerteventura is wonderful. *A12*

3 PLAYAS DE PAPAGAYO ★ ✲

3–5km east of Playa Blanca / 15 mins by car via the LZ 702, then bumpy road, or 30 mins by water taxi/excursion boat

Framed by rocks, the island's paradise beaches here are covered with fine, golden sand; the turquoise water is beautifully clean. In addition, the currents are usually weak and the waves gentle, so that children can safely swim and paddle.

The beaches are only accessible by car via a signposted track *(3 euros)*. The admission charge also includes entry to the nature reserve, the *Monumento Natural de los Ajaches*, to which the beaches belong. Large car parks are to be found near Playa Mujeres, above Playa Papagayo and by the wilder Playa Caleta del Congrio. The Papagayo beaches can easily be reached in only 15 minutes on foot from the district of Las Coloradas. ➤ Park on the road in front of the Papagayo Arena Hotel and follow the signposted footpath to the south.

INSIDER TIP
To the beach on foot
This way you avoid the rough track and save 3 euros.

All beaches are easy to access, even the highly recommended smaller ones: Playa del Pozo, Playa de la Cera and Playa de Puerto Muelas. When the tide is out, you can walk from one beach to the next. *B12*

4 FEMÉS ★

9km northeast of Playa Blanca / 10 mins by car via the LZ 702

The name, *Balcón de Femés*, is fully justified. If the weather is fine, from this pass at 450m you get an amazing view over the Rubicón plain, far beyond Playa Blanca and across to Isla de Lobos and Fuerteventura.

Femés is not much more than a cluster of houses, but the village can boast three decent restaurants. Eat in the *Balcón de Femés (daily | tel. 928 11 36 18 | $$)* directly at the viewing platform. The *Casa Emiliano (closed Mon | tel. 928 83 02 23 | $$)*, on the other hand, is set back a little, but has superb food and a pretty terrace. The *Restaurante Femés (daily | $)* is on the plaza. There is no view, but the locals eat here. Try the goat's cheese from Femés. ☛ Before you decide which kind to choose, you can try free samples at the small *Quesería de Rubicón (Mon–Sat 10am–8pm, Sun 10am–3pm | Plaza de San Marcial 3)* in the shadow of the church with a sip of

The Salinas de Janubio create an eye-catching pattern in the arid surroundings

wine from their own bodega. *€€)* you have an extensive view over the salt pans. The colours are beautiful at sunset!
📖 B10–11

5 SALINAS DE JANUBIO ⭐ 🏳

10km north of Playa Blanca / 10 mins by car via the LZ 701/ LZ 703

Forming long rows of rectangular fields in varying sizes in iridescent browns, reds, greys and blacks and resembling a giant patchwork quilt, the Janubio saltworks are situated below the road to Playa Blanca. Sea salt used to be of vital importance for the fishing community, as it was needed to conserve the precious catch – and their own provisions. Wind pumps, which have fallen into disrepair, pumped the seawater up 40m into the largest basins. From there it was gradually discharged into the smallest basins, after undergoing a series of ingenious evaporation stages. The workers then collected the crystallised salt into mounds using wooden rakes.

During the 19th century, the salt pans still yielded more than 10,000 tons of salt every year. Only small quantities are harvested now. You can buy this tasty coarse sea salt on the edge of the salt fields at *Bodega de Janubio (Mon–Fri 10am–5pm, Sat 11am–4pm | LZ 703, Km2 | salinas dejanubio.com)*. Unlike industrial salt, which is produced in large vacuum evaporation plants, sea salt is a purely natural product harvested manually. It is rich in calcium, magnesium and iodine as it retains all its minerals. From the *Mirador Las Salinas Casa Domingo* restaurant *(daily 11am–9pm | C/ Hervidero 7 | tel. 928 17 30 70 |*

The food is excellent as well – how about *pescado a la sal*, fish baked gently in a salt crust? After your meal you can walk over the lava beach below the saltworks and get a closer look at the salt flats. *📖 A–B10*

6 LOS HERVIDEROS ⭐

12km north of Playa Blanca / 10 mins by car via the LZ 701/ LZ 703

The water bubbles and hisses at Los Hervideros (Boiling Waters), which lie between Salinas de Janubio and El Golfo. This impressive spectacle of caves and arches has occurred through tidal erosion of the porous lava rock. At high tide, and especially when heavy swells roll in, the water crashes through them and up into the air with great force. A set of angled paths and staircases lead to a viewing platform amidst the mêlée. A surfaced car park is located at the side. *📖 A10*

7 EL GOLFO & CHARCO DE LOS CLICOS ⭐

16km north of Playa Blanca / 15 mins by car via the LZ 701/LZ 703)

Like the Fire Mountains, the deep green lagoon, *Charco de los Clicos (admission fee planned)*, has featured in a science-fiction movie. Shaped like a sickle, the lake fills a sunken volcanic crater, half of which is in a cove by the sea. The walls of the crater have been eroded by wind. What makes this lake such an attraction is the unusual colour of the water. Sea water, which after evaporation has a higher salt content, remains trapped in the crater and, due to special algae, then turns a bright green. The contrast with the tar-black lava sand, the dark blue Atlantic and the white spray is striking. Access on foot: from the car park by the country lane to the south of the lagoon and from the car park on the left at the edge of the village of El Golfo.

The country lane ends on the other side of the lagoon in the fishing village of *El Golfo*. It's perhaps hard to believe, but the entire village, together with hotel and restaurants, is threatened with demolition. According to Spanish law, houses less than 100m from the sea at low tide are illegal. As houses in similar coastal locations elsewhere in the Canaries have been summarily torn down, the inhabitants of El Golfo fear the worst.

Despite the threat hanging over the village, it can still boast some of the best fish restaurants in Lanzarote. You eat on beautiful terraces by the sea. The best restaurants are *Lago Verde* (closed Thu | Av. Marítima 46 | tel. 928 17 33 11 | €€-€€€) and *Bogavante* (daily | Av. Marítima 39 | tel. 928 17 35 05 | €€-€€€). For the best value for money, head to *Casa Rafa* (closed Mon | Av. Marítima | tel. 625 10 43 30 | restaurantedemar.com | €€) with its small menu but large portions and good house wines! Make sure you try the desserts: home-made ice-cream in unusual flavours as well as the spongy, creamy cheesecake (tarta de queso).

🖻 YAIZA

13km northeast of Playa Blanca / 13 mins by car via the LZ 701

This is what César Manrique wanted to see throughout the island: gleaming white houses, bright green window shutters and flowering geraniums. Yaiza, Lanzarote's model village, has already won several "beauty competitions". One particularly harmonious ensemble is to be found around the 17th-century church of *Nuestra Señora de los Remedios* and the two adjoining squares.

It is worth taking a look inside the church with its exposed bells in the bell tower. The Madonna statue on the high altar is bathed in a mysterious blue light shining in through the church windows. Every year on 8 September the figure leads a procession through the village. Opposite the church is the low, white *Casa de la Cultura (Mon-Fri 9am-1pm and 5-7pm)*, Yaiza's cultural centre. Built in the 19th century, it was from 1871 to 1937 the residence of the Spanish politician and writer, Benito Pérez Armas, and is now used for temporary exhibitions.

Artworks are also displayed in the *Galería Yaiza (Mon-Sat 5-7pm | Ctra General 13/LZ-2)*, the beautifully restored former village smithy and Lanzarote's first private gallery (1984). Works by Lanzarote favourites such as César Manrique and Ildefonso Aguilar, Veno and Tayó are exhibited here and expressive paintings, virtuosic drawings and etchings are sold at affordable prices. Together with his friend Luis Ibáñez, César Manrique

Iglesia de Nuestra Señora de los Remedios

restored an old rural manor house at the heart of the village and launched the restaurant *La Era (C/ Barranco 3 | $$)* there in 1968. The destination offers attractive dining rooms, a richly planted courtyard and many pretty architectural details. For a long time it was the gastronomic jewel in the south of the island's crown and people still enjoy stopping by here.

At the opposite end of the village, the former school, the *Antigua Escuela (C/ La Cuesta 1/LZ 2)*, is also worth seeking out. Instead of classrooms, it houses a bistro-café and interesting shops selling jewellery and handicrafts. The range of goods in *La Route des Caravanes* is a scene from the Arabian Nights. *La Bodega Santiago (closed Mon | LZ 67 | on the road to the*

Fire Mountains | tel. 928 83 62 04 | €€), a quaint country inn, serves Lanzarote wines to accompany creative twists on Canarian cuisine – tuna carpaccio with marinated sea snails, langoustine salad with mini beans and the best fillet of beef. Ask Juan Carlos about his daily specials.

INSIDER TIP
Dinner under the fig tree

B–C10

🄲 UGA

15km northeast of Playa Blanca / 15 mins by car via the LZ 701

This tiny, oasis-like village with dazzling white, cuboid houses, palm trees and an African-sounding name is also home to the dromedaries, which trek across the Fire Mountains bearing day-trippers. When their day's work is done, they are usually to be seen passing the Uga–Yaiza roundabout (where a giant monument was erected in their honour) between 4.30pm and 5pm. Uga is also well known for its *salmon smokehouse* situated on the road to Arrecife (but be aware that the minimum purchase is 500 g). *Casa Gregorio* in the village *(closed Tue | tel. 928 83 01 08 | €–€€)* is highly regarded for its inexpensive and delicious Lanzarotean fare. *C10*

🔟 FUERTEVENTURA
15km south of Playa Blanca /
30 mins by ferry
You can see Lanzarote's big sister from anywhere on Playa Blanca. Would you like to meet her? It only takes 30 minutes for the ferry to cross from Playa Blanca to the harbour at Corralejo on the neighbouring island. It leaves on the hour from 7am and the last return crossing is at 8pm. You'll find a detailed description of a day trip to Fuerteventura on p. 112; and a full description of the island in *MARCO POLO Fuerteventura*.

PARQUE NACIONAL DE TIMANFAYA

(B–C 8-9) **Lunar landscape? Trip to hell? Bowels of the earth? At Timanfaya National Park you will feel as though you have just landed on a different planet. Its name is derived from a village that disappeared under the lava.**

Clouds cast bizarre shadows, the wind scurries across the plain, whistling between jagged chunks of magma, stirring up the tiny lapilli, the lava shingle that lies in layers many feet deep. These droplets of molten or semi-molten lava are known on the Canaries as *picón*. Not a single tree or shrub interrupts the monotony. It's a lunar landscape.

The *Montañas del Fuego*, Fire Mountains, evoke a degree of trepidation in everyone who visits this desolate region. Not least as one of the worst catastrophes recorded in the history of the modern world happened here. The volcanic eruptions on Lanzarote lasted for six years, from 1730 to 1736. They buried almost a quarter of the island and left behind the largest field of lava in the world. Many *Lanzaroteños* fled to Gran Canaria. Many places were either buried by clouds of ash or devastated by streams of lava that afterwards flowed on into the sea. Millions of fish died, only to wash up later along the coast. New mountains rose, craters were formed and exploded on the same day, chasms opened up. The heat burnt the fields and cattle succumbed to the poisonous vapours. In 1824 the peace was shattered again. Three more volcanoes were formed but the devastation bore no comparison to what had happened in the previous century.

Now everything has solidified. The immense power of the volcanic forces can be viewed and admired in safety. The LZ 67 road from Yaiza to Mancha Blanca crosses the forbidding *malpaís*, the "badlands" of solid magma. Rising on the left are the thirty or so cones of the Montañas del Fuego, among them the 510m Timanfaya, surrounded by equally impressive companions. The colours gleam in the sun. The fluorescence is caused by the different minerals in the lava. This collection of conical hills is part of the Timanfaya National Park.

From the LZ 67 a narrow asphalt road branches off to a cabin made from dark lava stone. After paying the admission fee, continue for another 3km to the *Islote de Hilario*, a vantage point rising from the flat landscape like an islet *(islote)*. This is also the starting point of the tours included in the entrance fee along the *Ruta de los Volcanes* (see p. 100). *Daily 9am–5.45pm | admission 10 euros*

SIGHTSEEING & ACTIVITIES

⓫ ECHADERO DE LOS CAMELLOS ⭐ 👫

The most exotic Lanzarote experience is to ride on the back of a dromedary through the black lava sea of Timanfaya National Park. One hundred animals await their customers at the "camels' berth". A small museum *(Mon–Sat 8am–3pm)* displays a whole range of lava rocks from the national park. *Mon–Fri 9am–3pm | tour 8 euros per person | ⏱ 30 mins | ▥ C9*

Experience Earth's raw power in Timanfaya National Park

Some areas of the national park are only accessible to camels and their riders

12 RUTA DE LOS VOLCANES ★ 📷

The highlight of the national park is the journey along the 14-km volcano route. It is not open to private cars; the only way to explore the park is a bus tour from *Islote de Hilario*. The tour goes deep into a surreal world, where it seems as if dozens of meteorites have struck the earth, each forming its own crater. It's a lesson in vulcanology: look out for the steep-sided *hornitos* (small ovens) or 100-m-diameter *calderas*. There are collapsed lava tunnels and huge ash slides. As the bus continues its journey through hell you listen to heroic music by Wagner and Beethoven, as if the landscape wasn't dramatic enough already! You will also hear spoken diary entries by

the priest from Yaiza who witnessed the eruptions of 1730 that changed Lanzarote so drastically. The tour is included in the national park admission. Avoid the overbooked lunchtime hours! *Departures every 30 mins, last bus 5pm|* ⏱ *60 mins (bus tour 45 mins)|* 🗺 *C9*

13 CENTRO DE VISITANTES E INTERPRETACIÓN DE MANCHA BLANCA 📷

A good 4km beyond La Mancha, the 🐫 national park's visitor centre emerges from the black lava almost like a stranded spaceship. Interactive panels, exhibits and photos offer plenty of information about the Fire Mountains. Best of all is the movie,

ART EVERYWHERE

For accommodation with a personal touch choose the small but lovely *Casona de Yaiza (C/ El Rincón 11 | Yaiza | tel. 928 83 62 62 | casona deyaiza.com | €€)*, which has eight suites grouped around a courtyard. The highlight is the house's underground cisterns, which have been transformed into luxurious lounges.

ONCE A HERMIT'S HOUSE

Another great choice is the *Casa de Hilario (7 rooms | Ctra García Escámez 19 | Yaiza | tel. 928 83 62 62 | casadehilario.com | €€€)*, restored by an eccentric art-lover. The pool terrace offers views out over the sea and the brooding silhouettes of the Fire Mountains.

INSIDER TIP
Bringing volcanic eruptions to life

which is so gripping you might feel as if you're in the middle of an eruption. Finally, a boardwalk takes visitors a long way out onto the inhospitable expanse of black clinker.

Also great are the 📷 free guided walks (in English): sign up at reservas parquesnacionales.es. If you're hungry, you can stop to eat at Manrique's ⚑ *El Diablo (€€)*, (Devil) restaurant, built from lava stone and fireproof material, with all-round panoramic windows. Even if you don't want to eat, look out across the dramatically solidified landscape of black valleys, purple cones and ruptured craters. Cooks grill steaks on a massive barbecue powered by heat from the centre of the earth, while outside park wardens demonstrate what is happening below the thin crust of lava: brushwood thrown into a shallow pit outside the restaurant ignites spontaneously; when a bucket of water is emptied into a pipe set deep in the earth the water hisses as it evaporates. At a depth of 10cm the temperature is 140°C; at 6m it's 400°C. *Daily, 9am–5pm | admission free | at LZ 67, Km9.6 | tel. 928 84 08 39 | tinajo.es/centro_visitantes_tinajo. php | ⏱ 30 mins | ⊞ D8*

DISCOVERY TOURS

Want to get under the skin of the island? Then our discovery tours provide the perfect guide – they include advice on which sights to visit, tips on where to stop for that perfect holiday snap, a choice of the best places to eat and drink, and suggestions for fun activities.

❶ LANZAROTE AT A GLANCE

➤ Explore a dark and shimmering lunar landscape
➤ Be awed above and below ground: caves and incredible panoramas
➤ Marvel at shimmering coasts and symmetrical salt pans

📍 Playa Blanca	🏁 Playa Blanca
🔄 200km	🚗 3 days (6½hrs total driving time)

ℹ️ If you plan to visit several works of art by César Manrique it's best to buy the reasonably priced multiple ticket *(tarjeta sin contacto)* from Bono Bus Lanzarote, see p. 117).

The Papagayo beaches also look good from a distance

VIEWS OF A NEIGHBOURING ISLAND

Get an earlyish start so you have enough time – 9am is perfect! *From* ❶ Playa Blanca ➤ p. 88, *take the LZ 702 towards the island's interior. You will first cross a dusty plateau, then the road climbs steeply up to the village of* ❷ Femés ➤ p. 94, located on the eroded slope of the Ajaches massif. From the viewing platform, you can trace the way you came and see the neighbouring island of Fuerteventura on the horizon. Make sure you try the goat's cheese at the Quesería Rubicón!

INSIDER TIP
Cheese, anyone?

From Femés, follow the road through the upper valley to the Yaiza–Arrecife road. Head left to get to the picturesque village of ❸ Yaiza ➤ p. 96, which shines like a green-white beacon against the dark landscape – an ideal place for a short walk.

THE IMPOSING FIRE MOUNTAINS

Then take the LZ 67 towards the ❹ Montañas del Fuego ➤ p. 98, the "Fire Mountains" in the ❺ Parque Nacional de Timanfaya ➤ p. 98. It pays to come early in order to avoid the crowds so that you can enjoy the magnificent landscape without feeling

INSIDER TIP
Night owls, watch out!

DAY 1

❶ Playa Blanca

8km 8mins

❷ Femés

8km 8mins

❸ Yaiza

6km 17mins

❹ Montañas del Fuego

200m

❺ Parque Nacional de Timanfaya

200m

Montaña Clara 256
Graciosa 266
Caleta del Sebo
Pedro Barba
Parque Natural del
Archipielago Chinijo
Caleta
del Sebo
Río
17
Orzola
El Río
16
Lanzarote
Cueva de los Verdes
La Bahía
de Penedo
Haria 15
18
Jam
del A
Pta. Prieta
La Isleta
La Santa
Caleta
de Famara
14
671
Peñas del
Chache
19
20
Tabayesco
Pta. Gaviota
Sóo
Mala
Guatiza
Parque Nac.
de Timanfaya
Tinajo
Teguise 10
1
21
Los
Cocoteros
Mancha
Blanca
Tiagua
12
550 20
13
Castillo de
Guanapay
Islote
de Hilario
9
10
San
Bartolomé
22
Pta. de
Tierra
Negra
6 5 4
8
Masdache
11
San José
El Golfo
25
510
7
Fuego
Güime
23
Castillo de
S. Gabriel
26
24 30
Tías
27
3
Mácher
Arrecife
2
28
Yaiza
ACE
Pta. de la Lagarta
Las Breñas
Femés
608
2
Femés
Playa
Quemada
Puerto
del Carmen
1
Las Coloradas
Playa Blanca
Playa de
Papagayo
Punta del Papagayo
Estrecho de La Bocaina

10 km
6.21 mi

6 Dromedary station

5km 7mins

7 Islote de Hilario

5km 7mins

rushed. The start of the lava fields is marked by wooden signs on which a small devil, the *Diablo de Timanfaya*, sits as if on a throne. Shortly after, you will come to the 6 Dromedary station ➤ p. 99. Don't be afraid to take a ride on these Arabian camels because you're sure to enjoy it. Afterwards, you will come to a fork in the road leading to 7 Islote de Hilario ➤ p. 99, which will bring you to the heart"of the national park. On the round -trip bus tour, you will get to see the most spectacular places in the Fire Mountains – there are black lava flows, cones and craters everywhere to look! Then you can grab a bite to eat for lunch at the circular

8 El Diablo ➤ p. 101 as you enjoy the views of the Fire Mountains. At the **9** Centro de Visitantes e Interpretación de Mancha Blanca ➤ p. 100, you can learn all about the mysterious volcanic worls around you.

FARM LIFE & RUSTIC ACCOMMODATION

You can also explore what life was like on the farms here in days past at the **10** Museo Agrícola El Patio ➤ p. 81. *Located in Tiagua, to the northeast of the national park,* this lovingly furnished old farmstead is nestled within a subtropical garden. The **11** Monumento al Campesino ➤ p. 80 – *southwards on the LZ 20* – pays homage to the farmers on the island. You can also buy traditional arts and crafts right next door. The hotel **12** Caserío de Mozaga ➤ p. 83 offers lovely rooms for the night on a lava flow.

INSIDER TIP
Back in time

OLD CAPITAL, CHAPEL & PALM TREES

The next day, *take the LZ 30 straight to* **13** Teguise ➤ p. 60. The old capital with its white houses, monasteries and churches is the most historically significant town on the island. Stroll through this treasure trove of colonial architecture that bustles with business on Sundays when it plays host to a large market – expect crowds and full car parks on these days. Then you can really look forward to capturing the magnificent views at the **14** Ermita de las Nieves ➤ p. 66. This chapel near the highest peak on the island offers an impressive view of the west coast of Lanzarote. *Now it is time to head down deep into the valley of 1,000 palm trees that turns into an oasis when it rains.* Nestled in the middle of the valley, you will find the pretty village of **15** Haría ➤ p. 67 with its quiet streets and squares. You should have no trouble finding a place to park unless you visit during the little market held on Sundays – then it's best to park outside the centre.

VIEWS & LAVA TUNNELS

After Haría, the LZ 201 climbs back up to the point where it looks as if the edge of Lanzarote has been sliced with an axe, dropping straight into the sea. From

8 Restaurante del Diablo

5km 9mins

9 Centro de Visitantes e Interpretación de Mancha Blanca

10km 9mins

10 Museo Agrícola El Patio

6km 9mins

11 Monumento al Campesino

700m 1min

12 Caserío de Mozaga

8km 9mins

DAY 2
13 Teguise

11km 27mins

14 Ermita de las Nieves

8km 8mins

15 Haría

9km 19mins

⑯ Mirador del Río

10km 10mins

⑰ Órzola

9km 12mins

⑱ Jameos del Agua

1km 5mins

⑲ Cueva de los Verdes

5km 7mins

⑳ Arrieta

8km 120mins

㉑ Jardín de Cactus

12km 17mins

㉒ Fundación César Manrique

6km 9mins

the panoramic windows of the ⑯ Mirador del Río ➤ p. 69 you can enjoy breathtaking views across the strait between Lanzarote and the island of La Graciosa. Fill up on some tasty seafood at one of the restaurants in the fishing village of ⑰ Órzola ➤ p. 57. *The route along the LZ 1 to the south will now become quite exciting* as you pass through a hole in the volcanic cover into the ⑱ Jameos del Agua ➤ p. 56, which is a system of tunnels that César Manrique transformed into a magical work of art. This underground world is also home to the ⑲ Cueva de los Verdes ➤ p. 57. On the 45-minute tour through the multicoloured cave labyrinth, you will hear the music of the spheres – and experience at least one surprise! *Afterwards, continue on the LZ 1 to* ⑳ Arrieta ➤ p. 55, which is a good place to take a break on the small promenade.

PRICKLY PEARS & HUSTLE & BUSTLE

It is also worth stopping in Guatiza at the oversized *metal cactus* that points the way to Manrique's ㉑ Jardín de Cactus ➤ p. 55. Thousands of these prickly plants have been artfully arranged in these gardens. Don't miss the former residence of the "great master" in the next village that is now home to the ㉒ Fundación César Manrique ➤ p. 54, a fantastic museum built partly within volcanic bubbles. The

Nature at its most dramatic: Los Hervideros

capital of ㉓ Arrecife ➤ p. 38 then awaits with its endearing promenade along the coast. You can find accommodation for the night to fit any budget. A good mid-range hotel is the Miramar ➤ p. 47, which offers sea views.

WINE TASTING & DELICIOUS FISH

The next morning, take a walk to El Charco de San Ginés ➤ p. 43, the town's pretty lagoon. *Afterwards, drive back into the interior of the island. The route through the valley of* ㉔ La Geria ➤ p. 79 is unforgettable. It is covered with thousands of recesses in which grapes ripen before they are turned into the wine that you can taste and buy in the bodegas. *Pass through* Uga ➤ p. 97 with its seemingly North African charm *to access the LZ 704 to* ㉕ El Golfo ➤ p. 95, which is home to a number of fish restaurants. Take a seat next to the sea and enjoy the fresh fish – an unbeatable ambiance at sunset! If it is not too late, *drive to* ㉖ Charco de los Clicos ➤ p. 95, whose emerald-green colour almost seems otherworldly. End the day with two more highlights, namely ㉗ Los Hervideros ➤ p. 95, where the sea swirls through the rocks, and the fascinating geometric saline pools, the ㉘ Salinas de Janubio ➤ p. 95. *Then take the LZ 701 back to* ❶ Playa Blanca.

㉓ Arrecife
25km 29mins
DAY 3
㉔ La Geria
4km 15mins
㉕ El Golfo
700m 5mins
㉖ Charco de los Clicos
4km 94mins
㉗ Los Hervideros
4km 11mins
㉘ Salinas de Janubio
12km 28mins
❶ Playa Blanca

❷ DESERT LANDSCAPES & MONASTERIES: CYCLING AROUND EL JABLE

➤ Places of worship and a colonial town
➤ A shimmering sandy desert – like a mirage
➤ A long dune beach at the foot of a cliff wall

📍	Costa Teguise	🏁	Costa Teguise
↻	78km	🚴	1 day (5–6hrs total cycling time)
📶	medium	↗	400m

ℹ️ Note: Start as early as possible to take advantage of the cool morning hours. Resume the tour in the afternoon after a swim at ❼ **La Caleta de Famara**.

THE LEGACY OF PIRATES & CÉSAR MANRIQUE

❶ Costa Teguise
5km 15mins

❷ Fundación César Manrique
6km 32mins

❸ Lagomar
3km 13mins

❹ Teguise
10km 48mins

Starting from ❶ Costa Teguise ➤ p. 52, *go past the greens of the golf course to Tahiche.* The large wind chime at the roundabout tells you that you are getting close to ❷ Fundación César Manrique ➤ p. 54, which gives you a good impression of the artworks of this famous *Lanzaroteño*. *A second residence inspired by him is the fortress-like estate* ❸ Lagomar ➤ p. 66, *which you can access via the slightly uphill LZ 10. After another 2km, you will reach* ❹ Teguise ➤ p. 60. Take your time exploring its cobblestone streets and squares. If you are up for a real fitness challenge, then bike up to the Castillo Santa Bárbara ➤ p. 62 (an extra 150m climb!), which is home to a Pirate museum.

PANORAMIC VIEWS & GOAT PENS

❺ El Jable
4km 13mins

Leave Teguise by heading north on the side road and you will soon see the sandy plain of ❺ El Jable *ahead – enjoy the fantastic vista stretching to the bay of Famara and the cliffs above it. At the* Urbanización Famara,

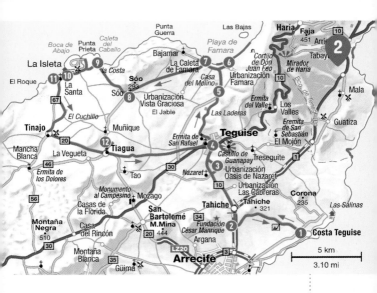

you will approach the coast. The sickle-shaped bungalows looking out to the sea that were built by Norwegians in the 1970s are sometimes referred to as "goat pens".

SURFERS' PARADISE

On the other side of the bungalows, you will find the ⓺ Playa de Famara ➤ p. 66, which is one of the most beautiful beaches on the Canary Islands thanks to its wild seascape at the foot of tall cliffs! Surfers ride the high swells here, but if you want to head into the water yourself, be careful because there is a dangerous undertow! The best thing to do is to stick close to the shore… *The beach stretches for 4km to the fishing village* ⓻ La Caleta de Famara, which still has sand-brushed roads and a seemingly authentic feel.

⓺ Playa de Famara
3km 12mins

⓻ La Caleta de Famara
6km 25mins

RESTAURANT BREAK

After stopping for something to eat, you will cycle slightly uphill to the sleepy hamlet of ⓼ Sóo. *Then the road sinks back down to* ⓽ Caleta de Caballo. The improvised weekend huts at the sea here do not really fit in with Lanzarote's more stylish image. *Next you will*

⓼ Sóo
3km 11mins

⓽ Caleta de Caballo
2km 17mins

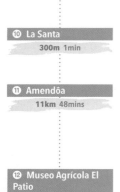

⑩ La Santa

300m 1min

⑪ Amendôa

11km 48mins

⑫ Museo Agrícola El Patio

20km 104mins

❶ Costa Teguise

pass by the mega sports hotel La Santa ➤ p. 83. In the winter, many racing cyclists take up residence in this hotel situated on a flat lagoon. The terrace restaurants in the town of ⑩ La Santa cater well to the needs of these athletes, offering freshly pressed juices and snacks.

INSIDER TIP
Refreshments

Although a little more pricey, Lucy serves up a particularly good meal at ⑪ Amendôa *(daily for lunch, only Mon evenings | Av. El Marinero 20 | tel. 928 83 82 52 | €€)*, offering an original fusion of Canarian, South American and European cuisine.

TRAVEL TO THE PAST

In Tinajo, turn onto the LZ 20 to Tiagua. Stop and visit the agricultural museum ⑫ Museo Agrícola El Patio ➤ p. 81. Afterwards, *follow the LZ 20 for a little bit before turning down a dirt road that runs along the edge of El Jable to Teguise and then retrace your steps through Tahiche back to* ❶ Costa Teguise.

❸ A HIKE THROUGH SEAS OF LAVA

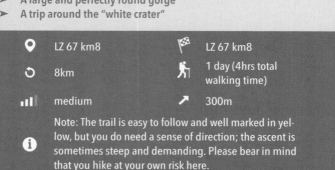

➤ Jagged and broken lava
➤ A large and perfectly round gorge
➤ A trip around the "white crater"

📍	LZ 67 km8	🏁	LZ 67 km8
↻	8km	🚶	1 day (4hrs total walking time)
📶	medium	↗	300m

ⓘ Note: The trail is easy to follow and well marked in yellow, but you do need a sense of direction; the ascent is sometimes steep and demanding. Please bear in mind that you hike at your own risk here.

FOLLOW THE RED ARROW

From Mancha Blanca ➤ p. 82, *follow the road to* Yaiza. When you get to ❶ Km 8 on the LZ 67, you will see the start of a lava piste – a sign marks the beginning of the hiking trail. Park your car about 700m away, at the end of the piste, which you can easily recognise thanks to the three big lava rocks *at the start of the trail* ❷ PR-LZ-19.

The path of the trail continues diagonally to the right, marked by a red arrow and a cairn. *For about 40 minutes, the trail follows a black lava flow. After about two-thirds of this stretch of the trail,* look on the right for the hard-to-find, but very pretty ❸ cave with particularly long lava stalactites.

THROUGH LAVA FIELDS TO THE VOLCANO

The red volcanic cone provides you with a visual orientation point for the first leg of the hike. At the foot of this cone and along a wall, *you will walk about ten minutes to the right and then another ten minutes through a lava field*. Keep the white cone of your next stop in view at all times. Once you come to the foot of the ❹ Caldera Blanca, *climb up to the left*, and make sure you stay on the border between the white rocks and the dark lava (approx. ten minutes). Then *hike for about another ten minutes to the right up the volcano,* make sure you stay along the trough that you were able to discern beforehand. Surprisingly, this fiery mountain is made of hard, light-coloured rocks covered with grey-white spots. Once you have reached the ❺ lower crater edge, don't be lulled into thinking that's it – *the trail over the left semi-circle steadily climbs an additional height of 200m* and takes at least 40 minutes. On clear days, magnificent vistas await at the ❻ upper crater edge (458m). *The descent leads to the right over the steeper flank of the crater and then you follow the same trail back to your car and the starting point of the hike at* ❶ Km8 on the LZ 67.

❶ Km8 on the LZ 67	
700m 3mins	
❷ PR-LZ-19	
1km 39mins	
❸ cave	
1.5km 25mins	
❹ Caldera Blanca	
1km 39mins	
❺ lower crater edge	
1.5km 43mins	
❻ upper crater edge	
5km 67mins	
❶ Km8 on the LZ 67	

❹ MEET THE NEIGHBOURS: HEAD TO FUERTEVENTURA!

➤ Wild West in the desert
➤ Weather-beaten volcanoes and rural traditions
➤ The finale: a great dune landscape

📍 Playa Blanca	🏁 Playa Blanca
🔄 270km	🚗 1 day (4 hrs total driving time; 1 hr return ferry)

ℹ️ Note: Don't forget your ID (also for children). It's better to rent your car on Fuerteventura, from Cabrera Medina/Cicar *(tel. 928 82 29 00 | cicar.com)* in Corralejo (see also p. 117). For more information, check out *MARCO POLO Fuerteventura*.

❶ Playa Blanca
35km 53mins

❷ El Cotillo
15km 14mins

❸ La Oliva
8km 26 mins

FISHING VILLAGE, ART & OPEN AIR MUSEUMS

Take the ferry at ❶ Playa Blanca ➤ p. 88 to Corralejo in northern Fuerteventura *(every hour between 8am and 7pm: Naviera Armas (tel. 902 45 65 00 | navieraarmas. com); Fred Olsen (tel. 902 10 01 07 | fredolsen.es); Líneas Romero (tel. 928 84 20 55 | lineasromero.com).* Half an hour later, you will see the shimmering dunes and attractive seaside promenade as you approach the harbour of Corralejo – but you should postpone a walk through the town until the evening. That way you can spend as much time as you want before you return to Lanzarote. *From Corralejo, take the FV-101 to the south through the desolate, sun-drenched landscape and turn right after 5km on the FV-109, towards Lajares.* It pays to make your first stop in ❷ El Cotillo, a friendly fishing village with two small harbours and an old castle. The next stop is the little parish town of ❸ La Oliva with some 18th-century buildings, including the Candlemas Church and the former colonel's residence Casa de los Coroneles *(Tue–Sun 10am–6pm | admission 3 euros | C/ Juan Cabrera Méndez)* which has an art gallery

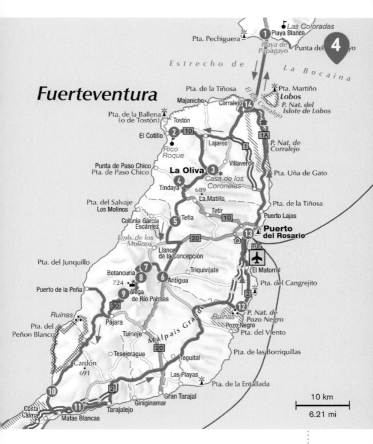

arranged around a courtyard with palm trees. You should also take a look at the Canarian art displayed in the neighbouring Casa Mané *(Mon–Fri 10am–5pm, Sat 10am–2pm | admission 4 euros | C/ Salvador Manrique de Lara). Then head further south* through the steppe-like countryside marked by volcanic cones. After passing by ❹ Tindaya, the holy mountain of the indigenous people, you will come to ❺ Tefía, which is home to an open-air Ecomuseo de la Alcogida *(Tue–Sat 10am–6pm | admission 5 euros),* a museum featuring restored farmhouses, mills and granaries. Another open-air museum with a beautifully restored mill and

❹ Tindaya	
	9km 7mins
❺ Tefía	
	17km 16min

estate *Molino de Antigua (Tue–Sat 10am–6pm | admission 2 euros)* plus a cheese museum *(Casa del Queso)* awaits as you approach ❻ Antigua.

❻ **Antigua**

8km 8mins

THROUGH THE MOUNTAINS FOR THE VIEW

Behind the village of Antigua, the countryside becomes more mountainous. *The road winds up over bends and bare crests* to the most spectacular viewing platform ❼ Mirador Morro Velosa at a height of almost 650m. *At the two gigantic figures* – artistic representations of the last ancient Canarian rulers – *turn left* and you will shortly arrive at a kind of country estate with a fantastic viewing terrace *(Tue–Sun 10am–6pm | free admission)*. On a clear day, you can see as far as Lanzarote, Gran Canaria and Tenerife.

❼ **Mirador Morro Velosa**

8km 9mins

SMALL TOWNS, ANIMALS & PLANTS OR SALT?

After some hairpin bends, make your way down to the former island capital of ❽ Betancuria. Despite the fortress-like cathedral, several stately homes and the ruins of a monastery, the town has all the charm of a sleepy village. Make sure you visit the Casa Santa María *(Mon–Sat 11am–3.30pm | admission 6 euros | casasantamaria.net),* which is an exemplary restored house with traditional craftsmen's workshops, a garden café and a restaurant. *After leaving Betancuria, drive past* ❾ Vega de Río Palmas, a palm tree oasis with a pilgrimage church. The appeal of the countryside grows even more as you look out over red mountains studded with furrows caused by erosion and isolated valleys in which hardly any plants thrive. If you have enough time, you might want to *take a detour from Pájara to the coastal village of Ajuy* (an additional 20km) because the contrast between the white weathered limestone walls and the black lava beach is amazing. *Otherwise, follow the seemingly endless string of valleys and peaks straight to* ❿ La Pared. White sand blows over the narrow isthmus that runs for 5km from here to the eastern side of the island. *Now you need to head north* to make sure that you catch the last ferry back to Lanzarote. Additional places worth visiting include the zoo and botanical gardens of ⓫ Oasis Park *(daily*

❽ **Betancuria**

6km 16mins

❾ **Vega de Río Palmas**

50km 41mins

❿ **La Pared**

11km 12mins

⓫ **Oasis Park**

45km 40mins

9am–6pm | admission 33 euros | Ctra FV-2, Km57.6 | fuerteventuraoasispark.com) in La Lajita, the salt marshes of the ⑫ **Museo de la Sal** (Tue–Sat 10am–6pm | admission 5 euros) at the Salinas del Carmen and the capital of ⑬ **Puerto del Rosario** with is lovely promenade along the sea.

⑫ Museo de la Sal
16km 17 mins
⑬ Puerto del Rosario
35km 50 mins

LAST BUT NOT LEAST: PLUNGE INTO THE SEA OR STROLL THROUGH TOWN

The last stretch of the route over the FV-1 crosses the dunes to bring you back to your starting point on Fuerteventura marked by white sand and the crystal-clear sea. Go for a swim or stroll through the old town centre of ⑭ **Corralejo**, before your ferry departs for ❶ **Playa Blanca** ➤ p. 88 .

⑭ Corralejo
18km 60 mins
❶ Playa Blanca

Traditional crafts are still practised at Casa Santa Maria Betancuria

GOOD TO KNOW

HOLIDAY BASICS

ARRIVAL

GETTING THERE

Lanzarote's airport, named – surprise, surprise – after the island's "saint", César Manrique, is a drive of between 10 and 30 minutes from the main holiday centres of Costa Teguise, Puerto del Carmen and Playa Blanca. Cheap flights are available from the UK and Ireland with Ryanair, easyJet and Thomas Cook (flight time from UK is about four hours). Flights with no hotel booking can cost anything between about 100 and 500 euros. There are no direct flights from the USA.

 INSIDER TIP
Ship, ahoy! If you can't or don't want to fly, there are ferries leaving once a week from the southern Spanish mainland port of Cádiz. The Compañía Acciona Trasmediterránea *(trasmediterranea.es)* operates a car ferry service to Arrecife. The crossing takes 30 to 35 hours and can cost 380 euros (one way) for a car.

NO TIME DIFFERENCE

Unlike mainland Spain, Lanzarote runs on Greenwich Mean Time, so visitors from the UK and Ireland do not need to adjust their watches.

GETTING IN

All arrivals from the UK will be required to show a passport, which must have at least six months' validity and must have been issued during the 10 years immediately prior to the date of entry. Children need their own passport. Check any other requirements with your airline before you fly.

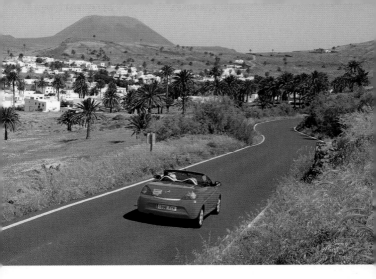

Sunshine, a soft-top and beautiful scenery – what more could you want?

GETTING AROUND

BUS

At busy times there are direct buses into Arrecife every 30 minutes (no. 22/23) and to Puerto del Carmen and Playa Blanca every hour (no. 161/61).

Scheduled buses *(guaguas)* leave for all the larger villages (but often only once or twice a day) from the bus station in Arrecife, *Estación de Guaguas (Vía Medular | near the stadium | tel. 928 81 15 22 | arrecifebus.com)*. All the main tourist centres are served by buses: Puerto del Carmen (no. 2) and Costa Teguise (no. 1) Monday–Friday every 20 minutes, Saturday and Sunday every 30 minutes; Playa Blanca (no. 6/60) Monday–Friday about every hour, Saturday and Sunday six to eight times a day.

A small, but much more centrally located bus terminal *(Intercambiador)* can be found at the western end of Playa del Reducto in Arrecife. Buses serve Puerto del Carmen, Playa Blanca and the airport. If you intend to use the bus a lot, you can buy a rechargeable *tarjeta sin contacto (Bono Bus Lanzarote)* which makes fares cheaper by ten per cent or more. The tourist information (e.g. at the airport) can tell you where to buy it.

CAR HIRE

Car hire companies have offices at the airport and in all the holiday centres. The cheapest local company is *Cabrera Medina (tel. 928 82 29 00 | cabreramedina.com)*, which also has the most branches and well-maintained cars – if there is any problem, they will provide you with a new car straight away. As the company also operates on Fuerteventura, you can also easily book a car if you plan to take a side trip to this neighbouring island (from the ferry port Puerto del Rosario). This will save you the cost of paying to have your hire car transported by ferry. If you book online, you can hire a small car (such as an Opel Corsa 3P) for less than 100 euros per week.

TAXI

Taxis to Puerto del Carmen from the airport cost approx. 22 euros, to Costa Teguise 28 euros and to Playa Blanca about 50 euros. All taxis must be licensed and equipped with a taxi-meter, which must be switched on before every journey. The basic charge is between 2.30 and 3 euros (depending on whether you're in the country or in the city), then 1 euro for every further kilometre plus sur-charges for night drives as well as for start or ending your trip at the airport or the ferry port. If you hire a taxi to take you on a round-the-island tour, make sure you agree a price beforehand.

EMERGENCIES

CONSULATES & EMBASSIES

Stolen passport? In need of emer-gency funds? Get help from the nearest consulate or embassy:

BRITISH CONSULATE

C/ Luis Morote 6-3° | Las Palmas de Gran Canaria | tel. 928 26 25 08 | ukinspain.fco.gov.uk

US CONSULATE

Edificio ARCA | C/ Los Martínez de Escobar 3, Oficina 7 | 35007 Las Palmas | tel. 928 27 12 59 | madrid. usembassy.gov/ citizen-services/ offices/las-palmas.html

EMERGENCY SERVICES

Dial 112 for police, fire brigade and ambulance.

HEALTH

It is easy for visitors to misjudge the physical strains that the change in climate places on the body, particu-larly at the height of summer. Tap water is not drinkable but can be used for washing and brushing teeth; all supermarkets sell mineral water in plastic bottles of 5 to 8 litres.

Emergency medical treatment is free of charge if you present the European Health Insurance Card (EHIC) or the Global Health Insurance Card (GHIC) issued by the UK govern-ment. However, in practice, doctors are sometimes reluctant to provide this free treatment. It is advisable to take out international health insur-ance. When paying for medical care, ask for a detailed invoice (factura), which you can present to your insur-ance company when you return home.

Pharmacies (farmacias) are recog-nisable by the green cross outside. Opening times are Mon–Fri 9am–1.30pm and 4–8.30 pm, Sat 9am–1pm. The sign with the words "Farmacia de Guardia" refers to the nearest pharmacy open for emergencies.

FESTIVALS & EVENTS
ALL YEAR ROUND

JANUARY
Los Reyes Magos (Arrecife and others): The Three Kings ride through towns and villages on dromedaries, receiving an enthusiastic welcome from children waiting excitedly for presents

FEBRUARY/MARCH
Carnaval The wildest celebration of all starts at the end of January and can go on until early March. Every place has its own dates for festivities and processions. The highlights are the events in Puerto del Carmen, Haría and Arrecife

MARCH/APRIL
Semana Santa (Arrecife): Holy Week processions are extravagant affairs

MAY
Ironman Lanzarote (photo; Arrecife): *ironmanlanzarote.com*

24 JUNE
Fiesta de San Juan (Haría): Festival to celebrate the harvest and summer solstice. On the eve of the fiesta campfires are lit and scarecrows burnt

JULY
Wine festivals (Masdache and other places in La Geria)
Fiesta de San Marcial del Rubicón (Femés): A week of processions honouring Lanzarote's patron saint
Fiesta de Nuestra Señora del Carmen (Playa Blanca, Puerto del Carmen, La Graciosa): Processions on 16 July for the patron saint of fishermen

SEPTEMBER
Fiesta de la Virgen de los Remedios (Yaiza): Processions on 8 September in honour of Yaiza's patron saint.
Virgen de los Dolores (Mancha Blanca): Festival on 15 September in honour of Our Lady of Sorrows

24 DECEMBER
Fiesta de los Ranchos de Pascua (Teguise): Folklore and music
Nativity scene (Yaiza)

ESSENTIALS

ACCOMMODATION

From five-star hotels to inns and from simple apartments to luxury villas, Lanzarote offers a wide range of accommodation. This is not only true for the tourist resorts, but is becoming more common in the interior of the island as well. *Turismo rural* is an option on a weekly basis in historic country houses *(casas rurales)* with all the amenities – perfect for families. A rental car is an absolute must for getting around because bus services are few and far between when you get away from the tourist hubs.

There are also a large number of privately owned rentals, but rates are now on par with those of hotels or apartments. It's worth being aware that there is local opposition to these *viviendas vacacionales* (private vacation homes) on the Canary Islands, because they mean that little affordable living space is left for the "normal" population.

Make sure you book your accommodation well in advance as the Canary Islands have become very popular in recent years.

Camping is another option and can even be free of charge 🐷, but the sites often fill up during the Spanish holidays: *Camping de Papagayo (Playa de Puerto Muelas | you must reserve ahead by phone: 928 17 37 24)*, is open June to September and at Easter. On the neighbouring island of La Graciosa, to the south of Caleta del Sebo, there is a campsite on the Bahía de El Salado with showers and toilets. Information and an online reservation form (two months in advance at the earliest) can be found at *reservas parquesnacionales.es/Isla de La Graciosa.*

HOW MUCH DOES IT COST?

Meal	*8 euros*
	for a dish of the day
Coffee	*1.50 euros*
	for a cortado
Beer	*2 euros*
	in a local bar
Wine	*from 7 euros*
	for half a litre
Sun lounger	*8 euros*
	for a day
Petrol	*1.50–1.60 euros*
	for 1 litre super
	unleaded
Aloe vera	*16 euros*
	for 250 ml

BEACHES

The beaches at the holiday resorts are well equipped: you can rent umbrellas and loungers, lifeguards keep a watchful eye on the water fun and there is a local Red Cross Station for emergencies. Free foot showers and toilets are provided and the next bar or café is never far away. However, things are very different at the so-called "natural beaches" outside the resorts – most don't even provide a lifebelt.

Please note that the currents and surf on the western side of the island are dangerously strong, which is why you should do no more than dip your toes in the sea. However, treacherous waves and unexpected rip currents can also develop on the calmer eastern side of the island. Be sure to pay attention to the warning flags. It's also worth knowing that nudism is practised on the more secluded beaches of Playas de Papagayo and at the Charco del Palo nudist resort (charcodelpalo.com).

CUSTOMS

INSIDER TIP
Less taxing

The Canary Islands have a special duty-free tax status. For this reason there are restrictions on goods you can take home with you. The limits are: 200 cigarettes, 25 cigars or 250g of other tobacco products. 1 litre of spirits and 2 litres of fortified wine (such as sherry or port), sparkling wine or any other drink that is less than 22% volume. In addition, you may bring back 1 litre of beer or 4 litres of still wine as well as other goods up to the value of 430 euros (children under 15: 175 euros). Check online before leaving home. For tax and duty on goods brought to the UK from the EU see: hmrc.gov.uk /customs/arriving/arrivingeu.htm

INFORMATION

Brochures, maps and other information are available at the tourist offices in Arrecife, Puerto del Carmen, Playa Blanca, Costa Teguise and Teguise, as well as at the airport. The website turismolanzarote.com has information on nature, culture, beaches and the sea, as well as sports and local events.

Lizard in Timanfayo National Park

LANGUAGE

You can get by without knowing any Spanish if you stay at a hotel in one of the tourist resorts. However, if you want to order something at a Canarian restaurant off the beaten track or even want to tour the island by bus, you should at least know some basic Spanish. For a list of useful words and phrases, see p. 124.

MONEY & CREDIT CARDS

You can withdraw money from ATMs using your EC card or any of the usual credit cards, but there are sometimes hefty charges. Many British banks have local branches or agreements with Spanish banks. Check before you leave home as you can avoid extra charges if you withdraw your money from them. Bank opening hours vary but most are open Mon–Fri 8.30am–2pm and Sat 8.30am–1pm. Almost all hotels, and many shops, restaurants and petrol stations accept credit cards. Some useful numbers to block lost or stolen credit cards are: Visa tel. 900 99 1124; MasterCard t*el. 900 822 756.*

PUBLIC HOLIDAYS

1 Jan	Año Nuevo (New Year's Day)
6 Jan	Los Reyes (Three kings)
March/April	Viernes Santo (Good Friday)
1 May	Día del Trabajo (Labour Day)
30 May	Día de las Islas Canarias (Canary Islands' Day)
May/June	Corpus Christi
25 July	Santiago Apóstol (St James' Day)
15 Aug	Asunción (Assumption)
12 Oct	Day of the Discovery of America
1 Nov	Todos los Santos (All Saints)
6 Dec	Constitution Day
8 Dec	Inmaculada Concepción (Festival of the Immaculate Conception)
25 Dec	Navidad (Christmas)

POST

You can buy stamps *(sellos)* at post offices *(correos)* and in newsagents/ tobacconists *(estancos)*. Sending a letter *(carta)* or postcard *(tarjeta postal)* should cost between 1.50 euros and 2 euros. There are private postal services alongside the reliable national company – these may be cheaper but are not always reliable.

TELEPHONE & WIFI

The country code for Spain is 0034 if calling from the UK or Ireland, 01134 from the USA, followed by the nine-digit number (including the Lanzarote area code 928). The country code for the UK is 0044 and for the USA it's 001. This is followed by the local area code without the zero and the number you are calling.

Almost all the hotels on the island offer WiFi or LAN internet access, but the price is not always included with your accommodation. Free public hotspots are rather difficult to find. Look for the "WiFi" signs in cafés and bars where you can usually use the internet for free as long as you order something.

TIPPING

If you are satisfied with the service in a restaurant, round up the bill by about 10%. Hotel cleaning and reception staff also expect a tip, as do coach drivers and guides on organised excursions.

Old postbox in Teguise

WEATHER IN ARRECIFE

■ High season
■ Low season

	JAN	FEB	MARCH	APRIL	MAY	JUNE	JULY	AUG	SEPT	OCT	NOV	DEC
Daytime temperature												
	21°	22°	23°	23°	23°	25°	28°	29°	29°	27°	25°	20°
Night-time temperatures												
	13°	13°	14°	14°	15°	16°	18°	18°	18°	19°	16°	14°
☀	6	7	8	9	9	9	9	9	7	7	6	6
☂	3	2	2	1	0	0	0	0	1	1	4	5
≋	18	18	17	17	18	20	20	21	22	22	20	19

☀ Hours of sunshine per day   ☂ Rainy days per month   ≋ Sea temperature in °C

WORDS & PHRASES
IN SPANISH

SMALLTALK

yes/no/maybe	sí/no/quizás
please Thank you	por favor/gracias
Hello!/Goodbye/Bye	¡Hola!/¡Adiós!/¡Hasta luego!
Good day/evening/night	¡Buenos días!/¡Buenas tardes!/¡Buenas noches!
Excuse me/sorry!	¡Perdona!/¡Perdone!
May I?	¿Puedo …?
Sorry?/Could you repeat?	¿Cómo dice?
My name is …	Me llamo …
What is your name? (formal/informal)	¿Cómo se llama usted?/¿Cómo te llamas?
I am from … the UK/USA/Ireland	Soy de … Alemania/Austria/Suiza
I (don't) like this	Esto (no) me gusta.
I would like … /Do you have …?	Querría …/¿Tiene usted …?

SYMBOLS

EATING & DRINKING

The menu, please!	¡El menú, por favor!
expensive/cheap/price	caro/barato/precio
Could you bring ... please?	¿Podría traerme ... por favor?
bottle/jug/glass	botella/jarra/vaso
knife/fork/spoon	cuchillo/tenedor/cuchara
salt/pepper/sugar	sal/pimienta/azúcar
vinegar/oil/milk/lemon	vinagre/aceite/leche/limón
cold/too salty/undercooked	frío/demasiado salado/sin hacer
with/without ice/fizz (in water)	con/sin hielo/gas
vegetarian/allergy	vegetariano/vegetariana/alergía
I would like to pay, please	Querría pagar, por favor.
bill/receipt/tip	cuenta/recibo/propina

MISCELLANEOUS

Where is ...?/Where are ...?	¿Dónde está ...? /¿Dónde están ...?
What time is it?	¿Qué hora es?
today/tomorrow/yesterday	hoy/mañana/ayer
How much is ...?	¿Cuánto cuesta ...?
Where can I get internet/WiFi?	¿Dónde encuentro un acceso a internet/wifi?
Help!/Look out!/Be careful!	¡Socorro!/¡Atención!/¡Cuidado!
pharmacy/drug store	farmacia/droguería
broken/it's not working	roto/no funciona
broken down/garage	avería/taller
Can I take photos here?	¿Podría fotografiar aquí?
open/closed/opening hours	abierto/cerrado/horario
entrance/exit	entrada/salida
toilets (women/men)	aseos (señoras/caballeros)
(not) drinking water	agua (no) potable
breakfast/B&B/all inclusive	desayuno/media pensión/pensión completa
car park/multi-storey car park	parking/garaje
I would like to hire ...	Querría alquilar ...
a car/a bike/a boat	un coche/una bicicleta/un barco
0/1/2/3/4/5/6/7/8/9/10/100/1000	cero/un, uno, una/dos/tres/cuatro/cinco/seis/siete/ocho/nueve/diez/cien, ciento/mil

HOLIDAY VIBES

FOR RELAXATION & CHILLING

FOR BOOKWORMS & FILM BUFFS

📖 MARARÍA

In this 1970s Canarian novel, Rafael Arozarena tells the mysterious story of a woman from the Lanzarotean mountain village of Femés who was very seductive but fell victim to a dangerous liaison. Decades later a stranger arrives in the village and hears the tragic story of beautiful Mararía (2009).

🎥 ONE MILLION YEARS B.C.

Thanks to Raquel Welch, this film has achieved cult status: the actress photogenically skipped through the Fire Mountains in a fur bikini (1966).

📖 DECOMPRESSION

A dive center on Lanzarote is the setting for this gripping psychological thriller about a murderous love triangle, by German author Juli Zeh (2012).

🎥 BROKEN EMBRACES

Los abrazos rotos, a film by Spain's star director Pedro Almodóvar, tells of power and passion and is set against the backdrop of dramatic island landscapes. Plus, it stars Penelope Cruz (2009).

PLAYLIST

0:58

II PEDRO GUERRA – MARARÍA
This Canarian singer-songwriter evokes the cult figure.

▶ ROSANA – LUNAS ROTAS
Rosana is from Lanzarote and sells records in the millions. Have a listen …

▶ BENITO CABRERA – NUBE DE HIELO
This timple player leads you through delicate to wild tones on the small stringed instrument.

▶ ILDEFONSO AGUILAR – EROSIÓN
Aguilar paints dark volcanic pictures with floating spherical sounds.

▶ LOS GOFIONES – SEGUIDILLAS DE LANZAROTE
Traditional Canarian music to move your feet to from the Canary Islands' most famous folk group.

The holiday soundtrack is available on **Spotify** under **MARCO POLO** Canaries

Or scan the code with the Spotify app

ONLINE

MEMORIADELANZAROTE.COM
Memoria de Lanzarote calls itself the island's "digital memory": the site records Lanzarote's past in text, sound and videos (in Spanish). Full of historical pictures to get you inspired!

MASSCULTURA.COM
Current cultural events on the island from literature to music and art, even for those without any Spanish.

DANISTEIN.COM
Photographer Dani Stein lives on Lanzarote and his blog showcases the island in incredible photographs – perfect for getting in the mood for your trip!

SAVE LA GERIA
This free app from the Lanzarote Wine Run details hiking and cycling tours as well as wineries in Lanzarote's extraordinary wine region.

TRAVEL PURSUIT
THE MARCO POLO HOLIDAY QUIZ

Do you know your facts about Lanzarote? Here you can test your knowledge of the little secrets and idiosyncrasies of the island and its people. You will find the correct answers below, with further details on pages 17 to 23 of this guide.

❶ Why are the Lanzaroteños called "the people from the rabbit island" (Los Conejeros)?
a) Fur is in fashion here
b) The island is overrun with rabbits
c) The former lords liked to hunt

❷ How much does a dromedary cost?
a) 300 euros
b) Between 3,000 and 5,000 euros
c) They're free

❸ Lipstick and Campari – but where does the colour come from?
a) Plants
b) Crushed beetles
c) A native species of lichen

❹ Where does Canarian wrestling *(lucha canaria)* come from?
a) Portuguese immigrants
b) Returnees from America
c) It's indigenous

❺ Who was César Manrique?
a) An artist and landscape designer
b) An important island politician
c) A famous dandy

❻ Where does the desert island source its (fresh) water?
a) It's brought in by ship
b) It's derived from seawater
c) It's derived from rainwater

Tending Lanzarote's bizarre vineyards is hard work

7 Which grapes produce the best wine on Lanzarote?
a) Riesling
b) Pinot Grigio
c) Malvasia

8 What are the "Couple of Mojón"?
a) A celebrity power couple
b) Fertility figurines used as traditional wedding gifts
c) A local breed of dog (male and female)

9 Who or what is olivine?
a) A semi-precious volcanic stone
b) A local olive oil variety
c) A popular Lanzarote rapper

10 How much of the island is covered with young volcanoes?
a) Between 1 and 10km²
b) Between 10 and 150km²
c) More than 170km²

11 When was the last volcanic eruption on Lanzarote?
a) 1966
b) 1824
c) 3000 BCE

12 Which Nobel Prize winner chose to live In Lanzarote?
a) Günter Grass
b) Albert Einstein
c) José A Saramago

INDEX

airport 116
Alegranza 69
Antonio Lemes
   Hernández 11, 65
Aqualava Waterpark 10, 91
Arrecife 38, 107, 119
Arrieta 55, 106
Balcón de Femés 94
boat trips 77, 91
Bodega de Janubio 11
buses 117
Caldera Blanca 111
Caleta de Caballo 109
Caletón Blanco 58
Casa Azul 55
Casa de Cultura Agustín de la
   Hoz 9, 42
Casa Museo César
   Manrique 67
Casa Museo del
   Campesino 80
Casa-Museo Del Timple 64
Castillo de las Coloradas 89
Castillo de San Gabriel 43
Castillo de San José 8, 44
Castillo Santa Bárbara 62,
   108
Centro de Visitantes e inter-
   pretación de Mancha
   Blanca 9, 100, 105
Charco de los Clicos 95, 107
cochineal beetle 20
Convento de San
   Francisco 62
Convento de Santo
   Domingo 63
Costa Calero 8
Costa Teguise 32, 52, 108
Cueva de los Verdes 8, 57,
   106
cycling 32
diving 33
eating & drinking 26
Echadero de los
   Camellos 10, 99, 104
El Charco de San Ginés 43,
   107
El Diablo 11
El Golfo 96, 107
El Jable 108
Ermita de las Nieves 66,
   105
Faro De Pechiguera 93
Femés 94, 103, 119
ferries 59, 116
Fire Mountains 98, 103
food 26
Fuerteventura 98, 103, 112
Fundación César
   Manrique 22, 54, 106,
   108

golf 34
Granja las Pardelas 10, 58
Gran Mareta 63
Guatiza 55, 106
hang-gliding 34
Haría 67, 105, 119
hiking 34, 59
Iglesia de Nuestra Señora de
   Guadalupe 63
Iglesia de San Ginés 44
Ironman Lanzarote 32
Islote de Hilario 99, 104
Jameos del Agua 56, 106
Jardín de Cactus 55, 106
La Caleta de Famara 66,
   108, 109
La Cilla 62
La Geria 28, 79, 107, 119
Lagomar 66, 108
La Graciosa 18, 58, 69, 119
Lanzaloe 9, 58
Lanzarote Aquarium 8, 52
La Santa 83, 110
Los Hervideros 95, 107
lucha canaria 21
Mancha Roja 93
Montañas del Fuego 98,
   103
Monumento al
   Campesino 80, 105
Mozaga 80
Museo Agrícola El Patio 81,
   105, 110
Museo Atlántico De
   Lanzarote 89
Museo de la Piratería 10
Museo Internacional de Arte
   Contemporáneo
   (MIAC) 44
Novios de El Mojón 31
Órzola 21, 57, 106
paddle boarding 35
Palacio de Spínola 64
Palacio Marqués de Herrera y
   Rojas 63
Parque Municipal,
   Arrecife 44
Parque Nacional de
   Timanfaya 98, 103

Playa Bastián 54
Playa Blanca 77, 88, 102,
   103, 112, 119
Playa de Famara 66, 109
Playa de Francesa 59
Playa de la Barrilla 77
Playa de la Cantería 58
Playa de la Cocina 59, 60
Playa de la Garita 55
Playa de la Madera 83
Playa del Ancla 54
Playa de las Conchas 59, 60
Playa de las Cucharas 54
Playa del Jablillo 54
Playa de los Pocillos 77
Playa del Reducto 47
Playa del Salado 60
Playa de Teneza 83
Playa Dorada 92
Playa Flamingo 92
Playa Francesa 60
Playa Honda 30
Playa Lambra 60
Playa Matagorda 77
Playa Quemada 79
Playas de Papagayo 21, 93
Plaza de la Constitución,
   Teguise 64
Pueblo Marinero 52
Puerto Calero 77, 78
Puerto del Carmen 21, 52,
   74, 119
Rancho Texas Lanzarote
   Park 10, 77
Ruta de los Volcanes 100
Salinas de Janubio 11, 30,
   95, 107
San Bartolomé 81
shopping 30
Sóo 109
surfing 35
Tahiche 108
Teguise 30, 60, 105, 108,
   119
Teguise market 65
Tiagua 81, 105, 110
Timanfaya National Park 18,
   98, 103
Timple 11
Tinajo 83
Túnel de la Atlántida 57
Uga 97, 107
windsurfing 35
wine 28, 30, 80
Yaiza 96, 103, 111, 119
Yé 69

Madsache 119
Microred La Graciosa 19
Mirador de Guinate 9, 68
Mirador del Río 9, 69, 106
Mirador Las Salinas Casa
   Domingo 11
Montaña Roja 93
Manrique, César 15, 22, 31,
   44, 52, 54, 57, 67, 69, 102
Marina Lanzarote 44
Marina Rubicón 89

WE WANT TO HEAR FROM YOU!

Did you have a great holiday? Is there something on your mind? Whatever it is, let us know! Whether you want to praise the guide, alert us to errors or give us a personal tip – MARCO POLO would be pleased to hear from you.
Please contact us by email:

sales@heartwoodpublishing.co.uk

We do everything we can to provide the very latest information for your trip. Nevertheless, despite all of our authors' thorough research, errors can creep in. MARCO POLO does not accept any liability for this.

PICTURE CREDITS
Cover photo: Jardin de Cactus created by César Manrique, Guatiza (huber-images: M. Ripani)
Photos: I. Gawin (131); Getty Images/AFP: D. Martin (20, 119); huber-images: S. Lubenow (99, 106/107), U. Mellone (front cover flap), Ripani (6/7), R. Schmid (43, 45, 88); laif: M. Amme (10, 26/27, 46/47), H. Eid (28), P. Frilet (100), G. Haenel (52, 121), J. Modrow (91), Tophoven (79); laif/hemis.fr: M. Dozier (82), L. Montico (34/35, 55); laif/robertharding: S. Black (56), J. Miller (75); Look: F. M. Frei (23); Look/age fotostock (2/3, 128/129); mauritius images: K.-G. Dumrath (14/15), M. Lange (38/39, 81), O. Stadler (64), M. Zurek (84/85); mauritius images/age (60/61); mauritius images/age fotostock: J.D. Dallet (Klappe vorne innen/1), N. Tondini (27); mauritius images/age fotostock/MAY FOTO (59); mauritius images/Alamy (116/117), H. Corneli (30/31, 76), P. Forsberg (97), A. Hartley (24/25), U. Kraft (126/127), J. Kruse (48/49), S. Meijer (9); mauritius images/a-plus image bank/Alamy (31); mauritius images/ib/White Star: M. Gumm (63); mauritius images/imagebroker: H. Corneli (92), H. Laub (32/33), M. Siepmann (68/69); mauritius images/imagebroker/White Star: M. Gumm (8); mauritius images/Islandstock/Alamy (19); mauritius images/Masterfile: F. Lukasseck (12/13); mauritius images/Prisma: R. van der Meer (67); mauritius images/Robert Harding (94); mauritius images/Spain/Alamy: S. Barnes (11); picture alliance/DUMONT Bildarchiv: S. Lubenow (102/103, 115); White Star: Schiefer (70/71

4th Edition – fully revised and updated 2023
Worldwide Distribution: Heartwood Publishing Ltd, Bath, United Kingdom
www.heartwoodpublishing.co.uk

© MAIRDUMONT GmbH & Co. KG, Ostfildern
Authors: Izabella Gawin, Sven Weniger
Editor: Petra Klose
Picture editor: Stefanie Wiese
Cartography: © MAIRDUMONT, Ostfildern (pp. 336–37, 104, 109, 111, 113, inner flap, outer flap, pull-out map);© MAIRDUMONT, Ostfildern, using data from OpenStreetMap, Licence CC-BY-SA 2.0 (pp. 40–41, 50–51, 72–73, 74, 86–87).
Cover design and pull-out map cover design: bilekjaeger_Kreativagentur with Zukunftswerkstatt, Stuttgart
Page design: Langenstein Communication GmbH, Ludwigsburg

Heartwood Publishing credits:
Translated from the German by John Owen, John Sykes, Susan Jones and Suzanne Kirkbright
Editors: Felicity Laughton, Kate Michell, Sophie Blacksell Jones
Prepress: Summerlane Books, Bath
Printed in India

MARCO POLO AUTHOR
IZABELLA GAWIN

"She's half Canarian," say her friends from the archipelago. "Plus, she knows our islands far better than we do!" Izabella Gawin was actually only planning on spending a winter in the Canary Islands, but her short stay soon became a love for life. She has written numerous travel and hiking books about the **Islands** and was awarded the "Author's Award" at Berlin's International Tourism Fair.

DOS & DON'TS

HOW TO AVOID SLIP-UPS & BLUNDERS

DO LEAVE THE PLANTS ALONE

Canarian plants such as *Euphorbia canariensis*, *Launaea arborescens* and *Asteriscus intermedius* are subject to special protection and must not be removed from the islands. Instead, why not buy a bag of seeds at the florists (*jardinería*) – it'll be easier to pack too!

DON'T CAUSE A BLOCKAGE

In many establishments, you will be asked not to put paper down the loo. The pipes in older Canary Island houses are narrow and easily get blocked. So please put used toilet paper in the bin provided – and the same goes for tissues, sanitary towels and tampons.

DO WEAR WARMER CLOTHING IN THE MOUNTAINS

As a rule-of-thumb, temperatures drop by 1°C for every 100m gained in altitude. Therefore, if the temperature on the coast is a balmy 23°C, the temperature on a 700-m summit can be a cool 16°C. And when you then factor in the generally strong winds on the summit, the temperature will feel even lower.

DO ASK BEFORE YOU EAT

Bread is a part of every meal in Spain and once upon a time it was always free. Today it is often placed on your table, even if you didn't order it, and then appears on the bill. It's a good idea to check if the bread is *por cuenta de la casa* (on the house).

DON'T SWIM IF THERE'S A RED FLAG

Every year, people drown off the coast of the Canary Islands, and often it's due to carelessness. If the red flag is flying on the beach, you must stay out of the water. Yellow means take care, and if the flag is green you can jump right in – although even then, take care not to swim out too far.